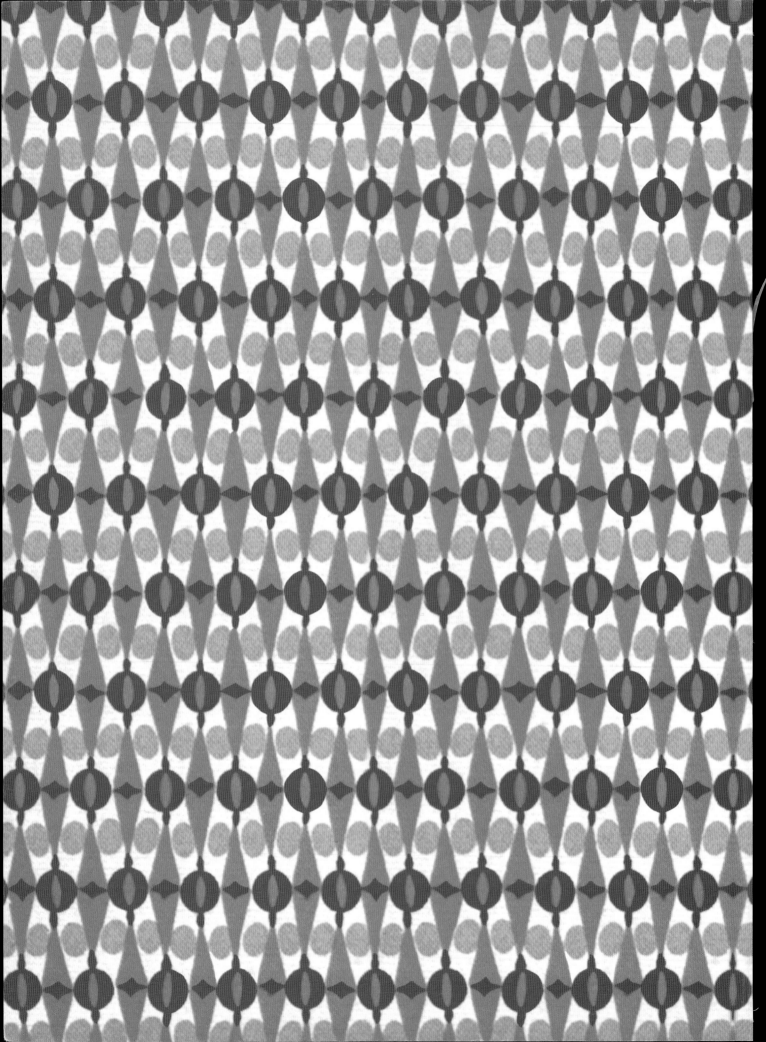

emma brennan

making **vintage** jewellery

25 original designs, from earrings to corsages

making
vintage
jewellery

25 original designs,
from earrings
to corsages

emma brennan

GUILD OF MASTER CRAFTSMAN PUBLICATIONS

First published 2006 by

Guild of Master Craftsman Publications Ltd

166 High Street, Lewes

East Sussex, BN7 1XU

Text and jewellery design © Emma Brennan 2006

© in the Work Guild of Master Craftsman Publications Ltd

ISBN 1-86108-453-6 (10 digit)

ISBN 978-1-86108-453-8 (13 digit)

British Cataloguing in Publication Data

A catalogue record of this book is available from the British Library.

Production Manager	Hilary MacCallum
Managing Editor	Gerrie Purcell
Project Editor	Clare Miller
Photography	Gill Orsman
Additional Photography	Robert Fyfe, Anthony Bailey
Managing Art Editor	Gilda Pacitti

Colour reproduction by Wyndeham Graphics

Printed and bound by Hing Yip Printing Company Ltd

Note:

Although care has been taken to ensure that metric measurements are true and accurate, they are only conversions from imperial; they have been rounded up or down to the nearest cm, or to the nearest convenient equivalent in cases where the imperial measurements themselves are only approximate. When following the projects, use either imperial or metric measurements; do not mix units.

foreword

Jewellery has been worn throughout the centuries as both a form of adornment and a sign of status and wealth. In the 1900s with the advent of costume jewellery fashioned from a variety of less expensive materials, necklaces, earrings, bracelets and brooches became accessible to everyone and remain a fashion staple today. This book aims to cover some jewellery-making basics in the introduction, and gives information and step-by-step photographs on the different techniques used in the projects that follow.

Fashion shops and galleries are currently full of jewellery to tempt us and with the resurgence in vintage styles and interest in beading and jewellery crafts on the increase, this book provides a wonderful basis for those wishing to dip their toe into a number of different jewellery-making techniques and materials to produce stunning, original pieces.

The main part of the book consists of 25 stunning projects, created using a mixture of these techniques. These range from wire necklaces and ribbon chokers to vintage inspired earrings and purses. Alternative pieces made using the same techniques are photographed with many of the projects to inspire.

My inspiration for the designs in this book comes from a variety of sources including my grandmother's tin of buttons that I played with as a child, vintage sequins and ribbons given to me by a lady who was a dressmaker during the 1940s and images from the fabulous home shopping catalogues of the mid 1900s. My love of textiles is also evident in many of the projects.

This book offers a huge variety of very workable designs and inspiration for fashionable, contemporary jewellery with a hint of vintage.

Emma Brennan

contents

1910s

1920s

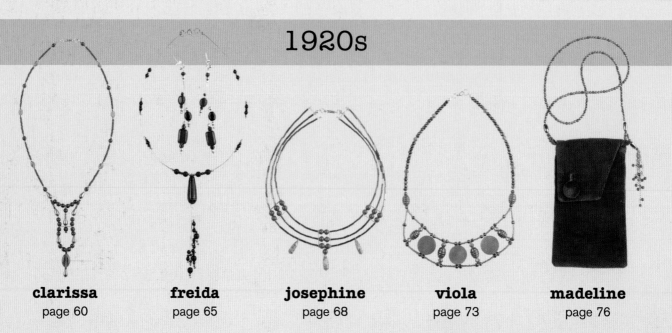

1930s

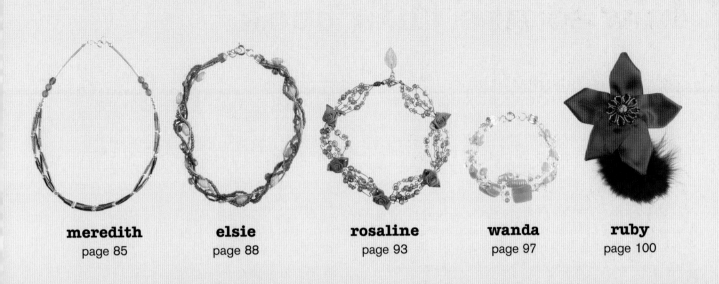

meredith
page 85

elsie
page 88

rosaline
page 93

wanda
page 97

ruby
page 100

1940s

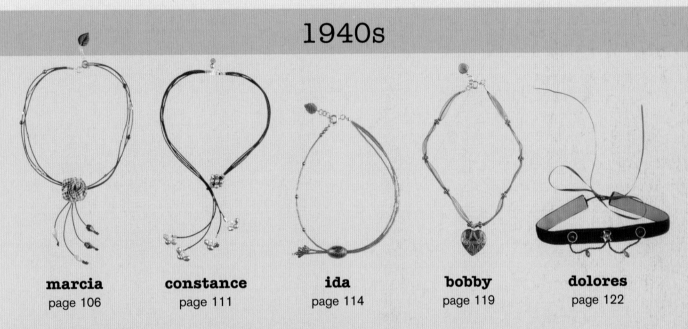

marcia
page 106

constance
page 111

ida
page 114

bobby
page 119

dolores
page 122

1950s

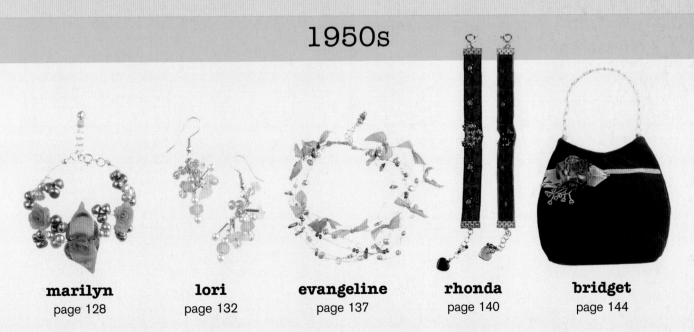

marilyn
page 128

lori
page 132

evangeline
page 137

rhonda
page 140

bridget
page 144

how to **use this book**

The book is split into sections. The first part of the book deals with the basic tools and materials required for jewellery making along with the basic techniques you will need to know before you attempt the projects that follow. The techniques are explained in step-by-step instructions and illustrated with photographs.

The 25 projects that follow are split into decade categories and have detailed step-by-step instructions and diagrams. The project instructions refer back to the technical sections in the introduction for more detailed help on things like attaching ends to necklaces. Where a project like a purse or corsage requires a paper pattern template, the pattern pieces given on the pages are drawn full size and simply have to be traced or photocopied and then cut out.

The 'era' categorization is not strict – I have placed particular projects within a certain decade because of an influence, shape or style detail – they are not meant to be historical replicas of period pieces. Each project will provide tips on how to vary the jewellery to give it a vintage or contemporary feel and how to adapt the techniques to make different pieces.

Many of the projects are straightforward and should be well within the grasp of anyone with some jewellery making or sewing knowledge. However this is not a 'how to' book for beginners and although the basic techniques are covered, many of the projects are meant to be challenging, inspiring and offer something unique when completed.

For many of the projects you will find pictures of alternative pieces and suggestions for using the same techniques outlined in the book, which will hopefully inspire you to create your own designs using these ideas as a springboard.

tools and findings

To make the projects in this book you will need the following basic equipment and materials:

tools See page 11

* Chain nosed pliers
* Round nosed pliers
* Wire cutters

findings See page 12

* Tiger tail wire
* Crimps
* Calottes or clam shells
* Jump rings
* Lobster claw clasp
* Bolt ring clasp
* Alternative clasps
* Ear wires
* Head pins and eye pins
* End caps and cones
* Spacer bars

basic **tools**

For making jewellery with beads and wire, there are very few basic tools that are needed. Essential kit is a pair of **chain nose pliers** (**A**) (also sometimes known as **snipe nose** or **flat nose pliers**)**,** which are used for a variety of techniques including opening and closing jump rings and chain links, making sharp bends in wire and attaching findings including flattening crimp beads. The pliers taper towards the points. It is essential to buy a pair with flat smooth insides to the noses – ones with ribbed insides will easily mar wire.

Round nose pliers (**B**) are also essential kit for working with wire. These have completely rounded noses that taper to the ends and are used for forming different sized loops at the top of head pins and in wire projects.

The third essential tool is a pair of **wire cutters** (**C**). These are used to make accurate cuts in specialist types of wire and beading threads. A standard pair should be suitable for most jobs. (You should not use standard wire cutters on memory wire, which is extremely hard.) All of these tools are readily available from bead stores or mail order catalogues.

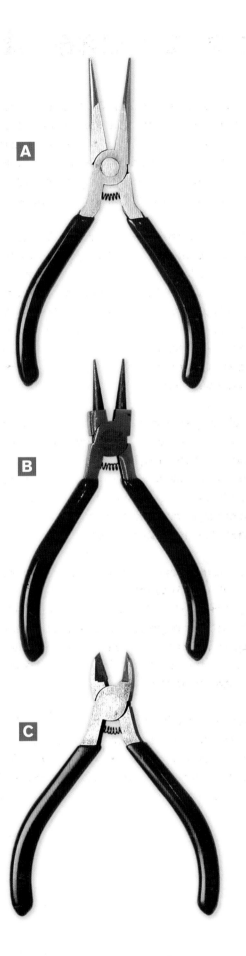

A

B

C

basic **materials**

stringing materials

Most of the projects in this book are strung on flexible beading wire, also known as tiger tail wire, or are constructed using fine craft beading wire.

Flexible beading wire or **tiger tail** (**A**) is made up of fine steel cables twisted together and covered with a plastic or nylon coating. Flexible beading wire/tiger tail is available in a variety of gauges or thicknesses and it is easy to string beads onto without a needle. It is also easy to use crimp beads with flexible beading wire because they grasp the plastic coating when squeezed flat with pliers. Less expensive varieties of tiger tail or flexible beading wires are prone to 'kinking', which is impossible to reverse. Some of the more expensive brands hang much better and can also be knotted.

findings

Findings are the metal pieces on jewellery that 'finish' a piece off or hold it together. This includes 'endings' for necklaces, metal rings, clasps, crimp beads and spacers. There is a huge variety available in different metals, including precious and plated, and with different finishes from plain to decorative.

Crimp beads or **French crimps** (**B**) are small metal tube beads, which are squeezed flat with pliers and are used to attach fasteners to beading wire. They can also be used in necklace or earring designs to hold 'floating' beads in place at intervals along the wire.

Calottes or **clam shells** (**C**) are used to attach fasteners to necklaces or bracelets. A crimp bead is attached or a knot made in the wire and the calotte closed over the top.

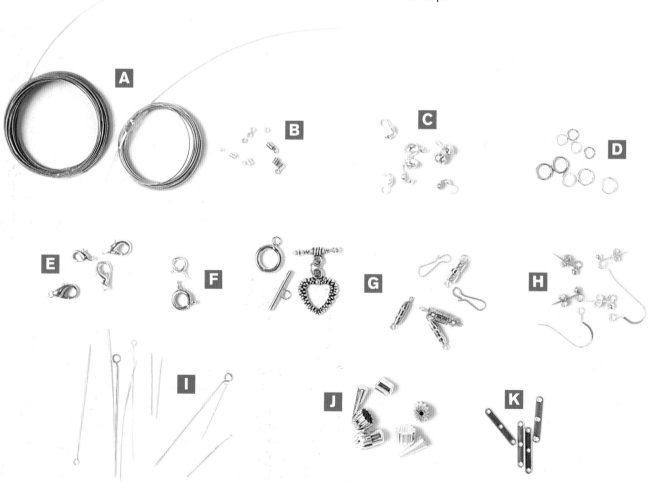

Jump rings (D) are metal loops used in conjunction with some fasteners. They are also used as links and to hang pendants from. Normal jump rings have a join which allows them to be opened or closed. You can also buy solid or welded jump rings with no join. These are used in several of the projects in this book.

Lobster claw (E) and **bolt ring (F)** are common types of fastener for necklaces and bracelets and are usually used with jump rings. There are a variety of other types of clasp available including barrel clasps, T-bar clasps and hooks **(G)**.

Ear wires and **ear posts (H)** are used to suspend wire and bead drops for earring making. The wire or post goes through the ear so it is advisable to invest in sterling silver or plated gold.

Head pins and **eye pins (I)** are metal pins used for making earrings and for dangles in necklaces. They can also be used to make support blocks in necklace or bracelet structures. The head pins have a flat head at one end, whilst the eye pins have a loop at one end.

End caps and **cones (J)** are used to cover knots or wires in multi-strand necklaces, bracelets or earrings, where the clasp or hook is attached.

Spacer bars (K) are used to space strands out on multi-strand necklaces or bracelets and for decorative design elements.

other useful items

Bead mat
It is useful to have a piece of velvet about 12 x 10in (30 x 25cm) to put your beads on while working **(A)**. This will stop the beads rolling around and the short-cut pile of the velvet makes it easy to pick up the beads on wire or with a needle.

Beading needles
Beading needles are long fine needles with narrow eyes **(B)**. These are very useful for working with beads because they are easy to pass through beads with smaller holes, like seed beads.

Thread
Projects in this book that combine beads with textiles use thread. A normal strong nylon-based sewing thread will suffice for these projects, but special thread made for beadwork, like Nymo **(C)**, is ideal as it is much stronger and less prone to fraying.

Glue
It is useful to have some non-toxic all-purpose glue at hand when making jewellery. A dab of glue can be added inside a calotte for extra security or on the ends of a ribbon choker before closing the end plates.

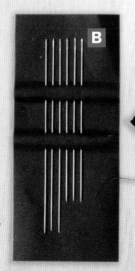

basic beads

Seed beads (**A**), also known as rocaille, are tiny beads used in beadwork, which come in different sizes ranging from 6 (the largest) through 8, 10, 11 and up to 15 (the smallest). They are used in bead-weaving techniques with thread or wire and are great for making fine multi-strand necklaces and for adding colour highlights.

Bugle beads (**B**) are small glass tube-shaped beads which are used to make fine strand necklaces and are also used in some bead-weaving techniques. They come in different lengths and colour finishes. They often have rough edges so are not suitable for using with threads that could be easily cut.

Semi-precious stones (**C**) are available in regular rounded-shaped or drop-shaped beads and in irregular stone chips or novelty shapes. A huge range of semi-precious stones is available from rose quartz to lapis lazuli, varying greatly in price.

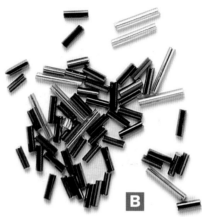

Faceted glass beads (**D**) are cut glass beads with faceted sides and include the very popular Swarovski crystals. They come in a range of sizes and colours and their regular size and shape makes them ideal for working with wire or thread.

Freshwater pearls (**E**) are real pearls which are available in a range of 'natural' irregular shapes and sizes, with different colour finishes.

Glass hearts, **flowers** and **leaves** (**F**) are glass beads that have been pressed into shapes. It is now possible to buy a range of novelty shaped beads, from less expensive Indian glass to genuine vintage glass.

As this book uses textiles and ribbons for many of the projects, I have included **vintage sequins and sew-ons (G)**. These can be used to trim everything from ribbon chokers to velvet purses and can even be worked into wire or strung as you would use beads.

Genuine **vintage beads (H)** can be sourced from thrift stores, antique shops and flea markets. It is possible to buy a whole necklace full of beads at reasonable prices. Internet sites around the world also offer everything from vintage glass to vintage Lucite. As the price of these can sometimes be quite prohibitive it is sensible to mix one or two genuine vintage elements with modern beads in a project.

Vintage buttons (I) are used for some of the projects in this book. The materials used to make buttons in the earlier decades of the 1900s, like glass and bakelite, means that they are often very pretty and highly suitable for use in jewellery making. You only need a few small buttons to make a choker or necklace and you could consider using single large buttons as pendants. Smaller precious glass buttons can be incorporated into wired centrepieces or trims along with beads.

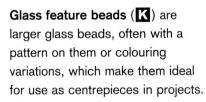

Glass pearls and beads (J) are inexpensive and are widely used in costume and fashion jewellery. Glass pearls are beads that have been coated with a pearl-like finish. These make a cheaper alternative to freshwater pearls.

Glass feature beads (K) are larger glass beads, often with a pattern on them or colouring variations, which make them ideal for use as centrepieces in projects.

making **vintage** jewellery

basic **techniques**

using end findings

Ensuring that the relevant end findings and fasteners have been securely attached to necklaces or bracelets is probably the most important factor in jewellery making. There are a few methods for attaching the endings. The following methods have been used for the projects in this book.

using calottes and french crimps

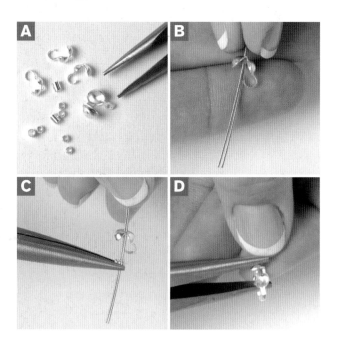

Thread the end of the tiger tail (or ends if you are using more than one strand) through the central hole in the calotte with the hook facing the end where you will attach the fastener (**A** **B**).

Thread one or two crimps onto the wire(s) and squash firmly in place using chain nose pliers (**C**).

Trim the tails of the wire(s).

Push the calotte so that it covers the crimps and squeeze it closed with chain nose pliers (**D**).

If there is an open hook on the calotte, close this into a loop. You will attach the clasp to this loop using a jump ring.

using closed-ring clasps and flattened crimps

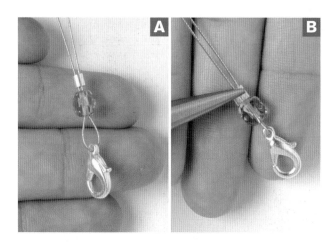

Thread a crimp and a bead onto the flexible beading wire. Take the tail through the closed loop on the clasp then back through the bead and the crimp (**A**).

Hold the crimp with the tip of the chain nose pliers and squeeze the pliers to flatten the crimp (**B**). You must be firm and make sure that the crimp is secure on the wire. Give the clasp a tug to ensure that it is secure.

making a loop in wire

Numerous projects in this book use head pin 'dangles' – head pins that have beads threaded onto them, with a loop turned above the top bead, which can then be attached to earring wires, chain links, etc. Turning a loop in wire is a technique that can be hard to master at first, but is used over and over again in jewellery making. The aim is to get the loop to sit centrally at the top of the wire rather than in a 'p' shape to one side.

Thread a bead onto a head pin or eye pin.

Trim the wire above the bead back to about ⅜in (1cm) and make a right-angle bend close up against the bead, using chain nose pliers (**A**).

Get hold of the end of the wire with round nose pliers and roll the wire over to form a semi-circle (**B**).

Let go of the wire, move the pliers around the loop a little, then continue to roll the wire until you have formed a circular loop, centred above the bead (**C**).

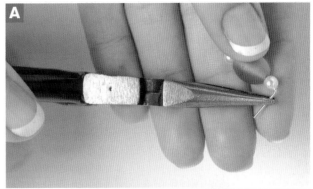

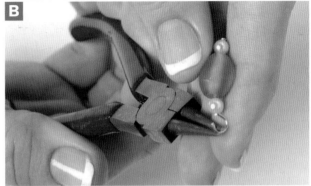

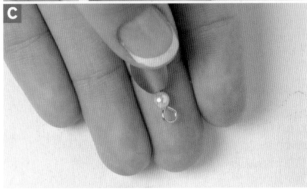

to open and close jump rings

Another technique that is required frequently is opening and closing loops or jump rings.

The best way to do this is to hold the jump ring with two pairs of pliers. Bring one pair towards you and the other away from you so that the jump ring is opened as shown in the picture from front to back rather than opening it outwards (**A**). If you open and close a jump ring outwards, the metal will be weakened and it is likely to break. While the jump ring is open, attach the fastener to your choker/necklace/bracelet before closing the ring (**B**).

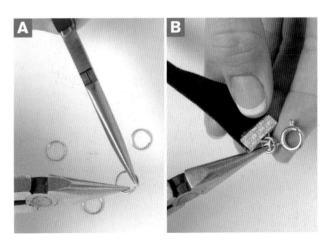

working with wire

There are lots of different 'creative' wires on the market which are suitable for making impressive jewellery that is also cost-effective. You can use plated or colour-coated wires until you've mastered the techniques. Once you are confident you can invest in silver- or gold-filled wire to make something a bit special, but for the purpose of practise, and making 'fun' jewellery, the cheaper wires are sufficient. Some of the colour-coated wires are good for making vintage inspired pieces.

wire

Creative wire comes in different thicknesses, which are also referred to as 'gauges'. The smaller the gauge number, the thicker the wire. Sometimes wire is sized in millimetres. Below is a rough guide to the equivalent sizes between gauges and millimetres:

Gauge size 28 = 0.35mm approx
Gauge size 26 = 0.4mm approx
Gauge size 24 = 0.5mm approx
Gauge size 22 = 0.6mm approx
Gauge size 20 = 0.8mm approx
Gauge size 18 = 1.0mm approx
Gauge size 16 = 1.3mm approx
Gauge size 14 = 1.6mm approx

tools for wire

To make jewellery with wire, you need much the same basic tools as you need for general jewellery making. It is essential to have the following:

✳ Chain nose pliers

✳ Round nose pliers

✳ Wire cutters

also used in this book

✳ A soft cloth for straightening wire

✳ A wire jig with pegs for bending wire into shapes (see below)

✳ A needle file, for filing rough ends off the wire

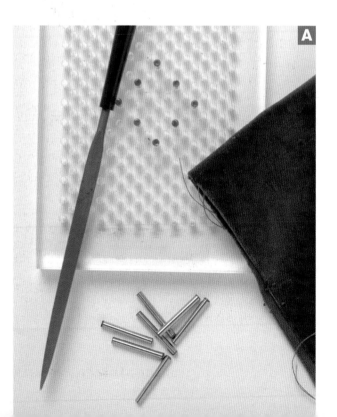

A

jigs

Two of the projects in this book have been made using a wire jig, a special device for bending the wire around, to form interesting patterns. Jigs are the best way to form 'regular' and repeated shapes. The WigJig, one popular brand of wire jig, is a patented device made from very sturdy, durable, transparent material (**A**). (Details of where to buy jigs are in the **Materials and Suppliers** list, page 154.)

working with heavier gauge wire

It is possible to make ornate vintage styled pendants using a wire jig, from which you can suspend bead dangles. The curved and flowing lines you can create with a jig are particularly reminiscent of the art nouveau style of jewellery. It is also possible to make everything from traditional Celtic inspired styles to contemporary and abstract zigzags.

To make bolder jewellery components using a wire jig, where the wire itself is a feature, including pendants, earrings and links, it is desirable to use 18 or 20 gauge wire. For example the earrings and pendant in **Eva** (right and page 55) and **Josephine** (below right and page 68) were made using 18 gauge wire. This is more difficult to bend round the small pegs of a jig, but is more visible and impressive when made up.

Different wires are now available with coloured coatings (generally the coating is made from nylon or baked-on enamel). These wires make very striking jewellery, but care must be taken when bending colour-coated wire, as the colour can scratch off.

Just to be even more confusing, wire is also available in different states of hardness. Most wire-workers use 'half-hard' wire. Without going into scientific detail, half-hard wire has been treated to make it more brittle. 'Dead-soft' wire is easier to bend, but offers no resistance, which actually makes it harder to work with. Most standard makes of craft wire are suitable for jewellery projects.

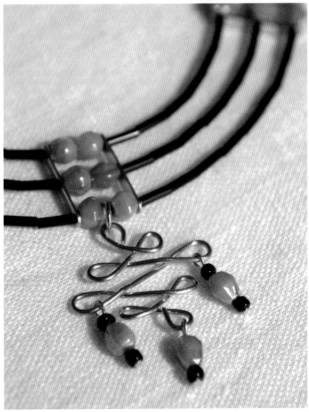

general techniques for using a wire jig

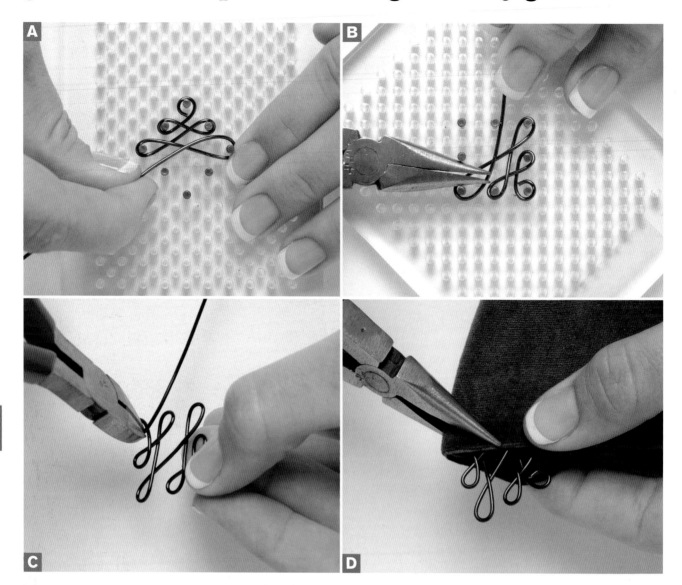

Place the pegs in the holes of the jig as shown in the pattern layout.

Make a loop at one end of the length of wire using round nosed pliers.

Place the loop over the start point peg in the design.

Wrap the wire in the direction shown in the project around the pegs of the jig (**A**).

Press the wire down against the jig as you wrap with your finger, a piece of doweling, the ends of the pliers or a file (**B**).

When you have come to the end point, remove the piece from the jig, cut the wire tail close up against the adjacent wire and tuck the tail in (**C**). File the end of the wire before tucking it if it is very rough.

Wrap a soft cloth around the piece and reshape it using chain nose, flat nose or nylon jaw pliers (**D**).

wrapped loops

For most jewellery designs a well-formed plain loop is sufficient. However, sometimes a design requires a loop to be closed, or have no gap in it. This is done by making a 'wrapped' loop where the tail of wire is left long enough to be wrapped around the wire stem after the loop is formed. Sometimes a wrapped loop is used purely for decorative purposes as a design element.

to make a wrapped loop

Thread a bead onto the head/eye pin.

Make a right-angle bend in the wire about ¼in (6mm) above the bead using the chain nose pliers (**A**).

Using round nose pliers and with the pliers placed around the bend in the wire, bend the wire around the top nose of the pliers (**B**).

Reposition the pliers and continue wrapping the loop around the bottom nose of the pliers so that you have formed a full circle (**C**).

Hold the loop flat with the chain nose pliers.

Wrap the wire around the wire stem in between the loop and the bead (**D**). Trim the tail close to the wraps.

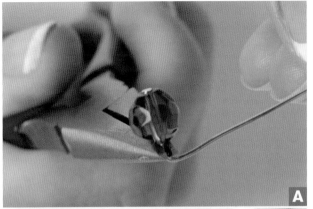

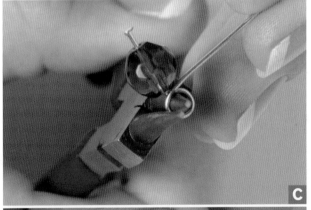

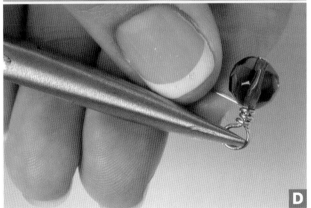

working with fine gauge wire

Many people are afraid of working with fine jewellery wire because it is more prone to breaking than the flexible, nylon-coated multi-strand beading wires. However, beads can be woven together with fine wire to make more structured elements for use in jewellery making. Wire has endless applications in jewellery design and can be used to make both regular beaded jewel pieces following a set pattern or for more abstract pieces.

Fine wire used in this book is generally 28 or 26 gauge wire. Like the thicker and heavier gauge wires, finer wire comes in a range of colour-coated, semi-precious and non-tarnish finishes. If the wire forms a major part of the design and will be seen it is advisable to use a non-tarnish wire.

general tips for working with 28 or 26 gauge wire

Be careful not to get kinks or sharp bends in the wire. This will make it more likely to break. If the wire breaks in many designs, you will not be able to rectify it by working in a new piece.

Keep the wire in large 'rounded' loops as you work; this will guard against kinks (**A**).

Do not 'overwork' the wire – this will weaken it and make it more likely to break.

In projects where you are required to make a loose knot in the wire, keep your index finger in the loop until you are sure that the knot is in the right place. Then gently tighten the loop into a loose knot (**B**).

In many designs you will be asked to cross the wires inside a bead. Remember to keep the wire in rounded loops as you work (**C**).

As a means of adding detail to a wire choker or bracelet it is possible to 'twist' the wire in an 'S' shape in between beads, using the round nose pliers. **Florence** (page 39), **Rosaline** (page 93) and **Wanda** (page 97) use this method. Grasp the wire with round nose pliers and twist the pliers in a clockwise direction, thus twisting the wire in an 'S' shape. Hold the pliers with the points downward and support the wires in the palm of your hand (**D**).

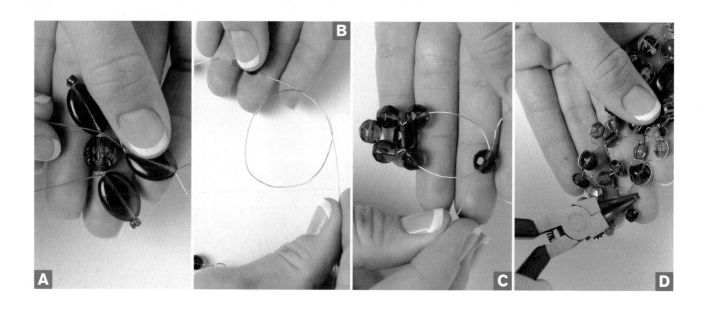

A B C D

finishing off with fine wire

With wire-work it is essential to finish off the piece well so that the ends of the wires do not stick out. Pieces can be finished in several ways. The easiest way to finish off a piece made with wire is to wrap the tail of the wire around one of the supporting wires two or three times, then to trim the tail back. This will suffice in most cases (**A**).

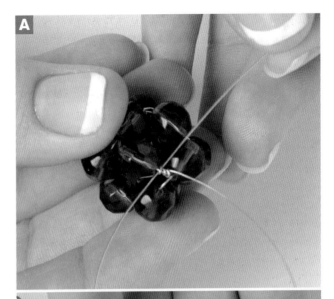

If you are making a pendant where the piece will be worn against the skin, it is advisable to try to hide the tail of the wire inside the hole of a bead after you have wrapped it around the supporting wire.

If wrapping the wire will show too obviously on a fine piece, then simply work the wire back through several beads in the opposite direction, providing that the holes are large enough.

On a necklace or choker like **Florence** (page 39) and **Rosaline** (page 93) which incorporate multiple strands of wire these can be finished off in two ways.

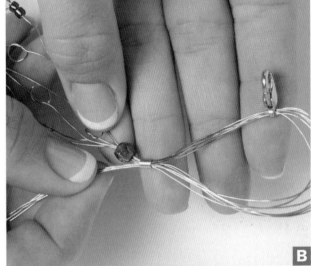

method 1

Take all of the wires together through a bead, a large crimp and the solid hole in a clasp (like a lobster clasp).

Then take all wires back through the crimp (**B**), and the bead if the hole is large enough. Take care and pull wires one at a time if necessary. When the loop of wires has been pulled up fairly tightly, squash the crimp, and then wrap the wire tails over the top of the crimp and around the supporting wires.

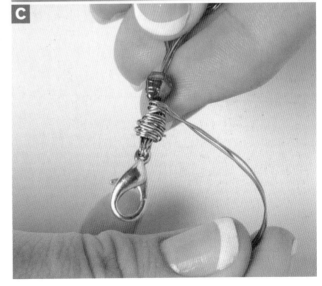

Trim all of the tails except two, then cover the other ends by wrapping these two tails over the top (**C**).

Cut the final two tails close up against the bead and hide against the bead.

method 2

Take all of the wires together through the loop of an eye pin and wrap them securely around the supporting wires and trim the tails if necessary (**A**).

Then thread an end cap or cone onto the eye pin to cover the wrapped wires (**B**) (**C**).

Thread a bead onto the eye pin the other side of the cap/cone, trim the tail back to about ⅜ inch (1cm) and turn a loop directly above the bead (see **Making a Loop in Wire**, page 17).

Attach the clasp to this loop, either directly or using a jump ring (**D**).

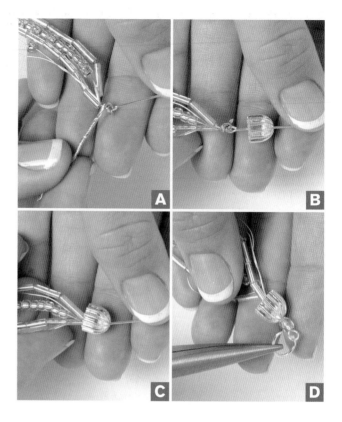

chain

The use of chain has become very popular again recently in jewellery making with the current fashion trend for 'charm' bracelets and necklaces. Chain comes in different styles and weights including 'curb' chain, which has flat-lying links, and 'belcher' or 'trace' chain, which normally has links at right angles to each other. Chain can be made from both precious metals like sterling silver or in cheaper plated metals. It is possible to buy chain that has an antiqued finish or copper- or brass-coloured finish, which is ideal for use in making jewellery with a 'vintage' feel.

Chain has been used in this book for projects where 'dangles' or charms made from head pins have been attached to the chain to create a fringed effect. Once you have made your head-pin dangle (refer to **Making a Loop in Wire**, page 17), open the loop from back to front as you would a jump ring and hook it onto a link in the chain. Close the loop on the dangle the opposite way (**A**).

leather and cotton thong

Cotton and leather thong offers a simple vehicle for bead stringing and forms a great base for many vintage inspired projects. You can mix it with organdie ribbon and a simple heart pendant as in **Bobby** (page 119) or use multiple cords to create a stunning lariat-inspired necklace like **Constance** (page 110).

Cotton and leather thongs are available in different thicknesses and colours. They are generally 1mm or 2mm thick and are used to thread beads with large holes onto, and for pieces where knots form a part of the design. Cotton thong tends to be softer than the leather and therefore the knots are less angular and it tends to hang better. I have used cotton thong for **Constance** (page 111) and **Bobby** (page 119).

There are special findings available that are suitable for use with cotton or leather thong, widely known as leather crimps, lace-end crimps or box calottes.

To attach a clasp onto cotton or leather thong, you can use a leather crimp.

Place one end of the thong inside the leather crimp. Add a dab of glue for security (**A**).

Use chain-nosed pliers to fold one side of the crimp over the leather (**B**).

Fold the other side of the crimp over the top and squeeze until you are sure the crimp has a firm hold on the thong (**C**).

Attach the crimp at the other end in the same way. Attach your chosen clasp to the crimp using jump rings.

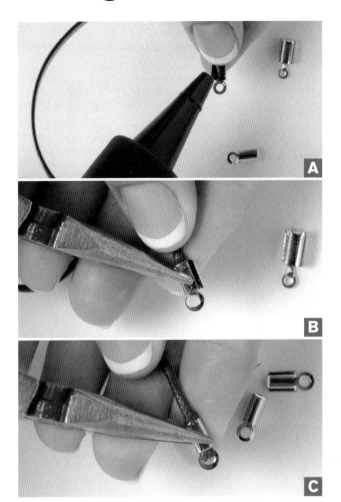

hints and tips

It is also possible to use flat leather in jewellery making, for example to make beads. The leather can be rolled up into tubes and glued in much the same way as paper to form beads. Small sized pieces are ideal for making beads and pendants as you only need a strip 1⅛in (28mm) by 3in (75mm) to make a tube bead. Good quality garment leather makes more delicate beads than the thicker upholstery leather. Leather can also be used to make the base for a choker, or to make flowers or leaves for corsages.

ribbon and textiles

ribbon

Ribbon has been used in jewellery making and for making millinery trims for centuries and was particularly popular in the 1910s and 20s. There has never been a more wonderful and diverse range of ribbons on the market as there is today, including exciting textures and weaves like velvet or jacquard, in a rainbow of colours. With corsages enjoying popularity again from the 1990s and remaining in vogue today, the art of ribbon work is enjoying somewhat of a revival. It is possible to obtain small pieces of genuine vintage ribbon and haberdashery to incorporate into fashion pieces like vintage inspired flower brooches or pleated ribbon cuffs. (See **Bessie**, page 45, **Ruby**, page 100 and **Rhonda**, page 140.)

Ribbon comes in different widths and textures which are suitable for different jewellery making projects. The ribbons used to make the vintage style jewellery and accessories in this book range from plain ribbon staples like grosgrain to the more decadent velvets.

Loretta, page 48, **Dolores**, page 122, **Rhonda**, page 140 and the variation to **Lillian**, page 36 (pictured above left) are chokers or cuffs which have ribbon bases. It is possible to use a single thickness of ribbon, but for the projects in this book I have stitched a backing ribbon to the main ribbon for extra durability and comfort.

ribbon roses

Ribbon can also be used to make tiny roses and flowers which can be used in jewellery projects. These can even be hand-painted with fabric dyes to give them a more antiqued or vintage feel.

to join ribbons together

Cut the main ribbon and backing ribbon to the required length (add a ¼in (6mm) to allow for the ribbon to pull up slightly when stitched) and place the ribbon wrong sides together with the backing ribbon.

Pin the ribbons together with the pins at an angle (**A**) then stitch using a short machine stitch down both selvedge edges approximately ⅛in (3mm) from the edge (**B**).

Press gently from the backing ribbon side to ease out any puckering.

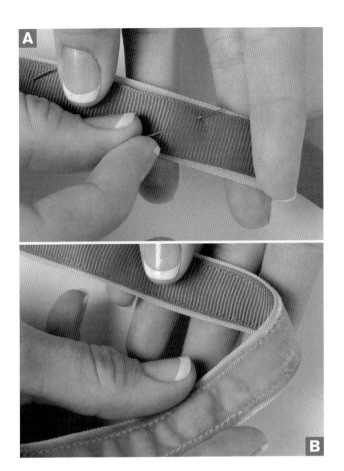

finishing off ribbon chokers and cuffs

The best way to finish off chokers and cuffs made from ribbon is to use special metal end plates. Most end plates have small metal teeth along the lower inside edges which grip the ribbon when squeezed closed. They also have a loop, to which standard jewellery findings can be attached. The beauty of this is that you have the option of using multiple jump rings or extender chains to make the choker more multi-sized.

End plates are becoming more readily available from bead stores as the popularity of incorporating ribbon and textiles into jewellery increases and are available with gold- or silver-coloured finishes.

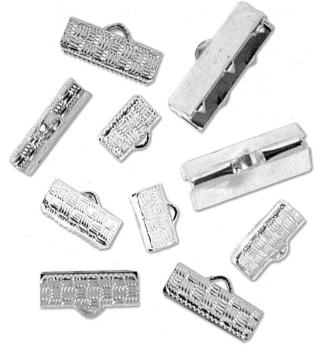

to attach the end plate to the ribbon

At one end, place the end of the double thickness ribbon choker inside the end plate.

Add a dab of glue, then using flat or chain-nosed pliers gently squeeze the end plate closed over the ribbon, ensuring that the ribbon does not slip out as you do this (**A**).

Once you are sure that it is in the correct place, squeeze it harder to secure.

You can then attach a clasp to the loop on the end plate using jump rings (**B**).

Repeat for other end of choker/cuff.

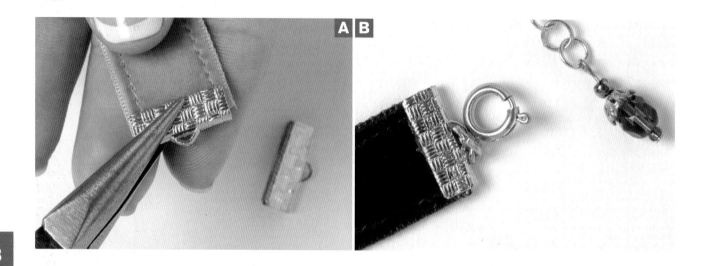

A **B**

hints and tips

If you cannot find the special end plates, you can always use a 3-hole connector, which can be stitched to the end of a ribbon choker or cuff. The advantage of using a 3-hole connector is that, as with the end plates, you can use standard jewellery findings, which make the choker or cuff multi-sized. If you are using a connector it is advisable to add a ¼in (6mm) seam allowance to the ribbon at each end, machine-neaten the ends and fold them over to form a hem before neatly hand-sewing them in place. You can then stitch the connector directly to the hem.

sequins and sewn-on elements

Sequins are a very vintage decoration and it is possible to buy genuine vintage sequins at specialist online beading and haberdashery stores. The great thing about sequins is that you need very few to make a real splash. You can now buy glass and plastic sew-on stones in a variety of shapes and sizes, again some original vintage ones.

One of the advantages of using ribbon and textiles for jewellery making is that you can sew various elements directly to the ribbon – you can use sew-on stones or sequins to great effect. Sequins are used in **Bessie** (page 45) to add detail to the centre of the flower. Sequins can be stitched in place using a variety of methods. The following method is used for **Bessie**.

to sew on a sequin

Thread a beading needle with a double thickness of thread; make a knot in the end and, starting from the back of the ribbon or fabric, make a couple of small stitches to secure the thread. Next bring the needle and thread up through the ribbon, sequin and a small seed bead.

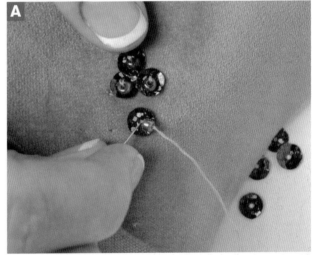

Then take the needle back down through the sequin and the ribbon. The seed bead will keep the sequin in place. You may wish to repeat the sequence for extra security (**A**).

beaded fringes

Dolores (pictured bottom right and page 122) uses thread to create festoons or fringes. For this it is advisable to use specialist nylon beading thread, like Nymo. Use a beading needle so that it will pass through the holes in the beads easily.

corsages and other textile projects

Ribbon is used in this book to make flower corsage brooches. The petals are formed from ribbon and are stitched directly onto a specially made base. Felt makes an ideal base for a corsage because it does not fray.

The instructions below are used to make **Ruby** (see also page 100).

To make a base use the circular pattern templates on page 45.

Cut out two corsage base pieces from felt and one corsage base from a stiffener like buckram.

Place the circle of buckram centrally in between the two felt circles (**A**). Pin all three layers together in the centre then, using a short machine stitch, sew circles together round the outside edge, about ¼in (6mm) from the outside edge (**B**).

Leaves, petals or beaded fringing can then be stitched directly onto the base (**C**).

Stitch a brooch backing bar (with holes) to the back of the corsage base (**D**). Always stitch it towards the top of the corsage to ensure that it does not hang down when worn.

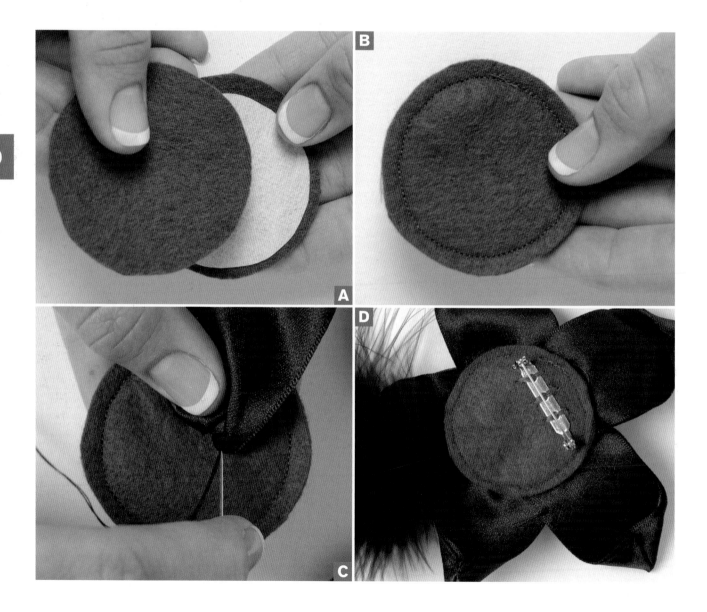

felt

Felt has long been associated with home crafts and its versatility, simplicity and non-fraying qualities make it ideal for incorporating into textile jewellery projects. Felt is made from different fibres. You can buy felt which is suitable only for crafts and is non-washable. There are now also felts that are washable, making them ideal for appliqué. The kind of felt used in this book is wool felt – it comes in a wonderful array of subtle vintage inspired colours and has a firm feel to it. You can also make your own felt if you are adventurous. It is possible to make handmade felt beads using dyed sheep's fleece. Seed beads and surface decoration can then be stitched directly onto the surface.

presentation

If you intend to give the jewellery you have made as a present, the vintage appeal can be heightened by your choice of presentation and packaging. It is possible to buy tiny drawstring organdie bags and plain boxes quite cheaply. Consider stitching a ribbon rose or extra ribbon tails onto a purchased bag to match the jewellery inside, or perhaps glue some vintage buttons or ribbon onto a box lid.

You could also make your own gift bags using inexpensive vintage inspired cotton prints trimmed with braid or perhaps you could make some tiny felt pouches for a more simple option. You can also print your own personalized earring cards (using business card software) on a computer. You could include vintage images or lettering, and possibly glue a piece of velvet ribbon or an organdie bow to the front.

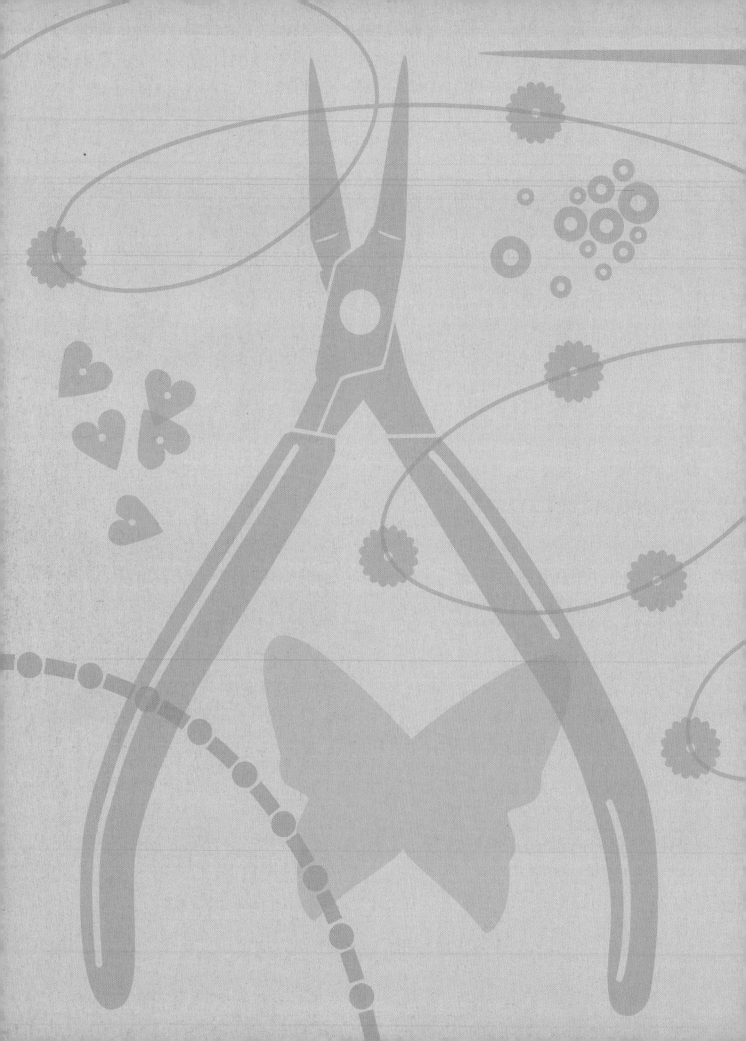

1910s

lillian

ART NOUVEAU FLOWER CHOKER WITH VELVET TIES AND MATCHING BRACELET VARIATION

In the early 1900s jewellery designers looked back to the 18th century for inspiration. Pieces were often influenced by nature and the popular art nouveau styles incorporated everything from stylized flowers to leaves and vines, appearing on brooches, pendants and earrings. Natural materials like wood and horn came into use instead of exclusively precious materials.

This elegantly simple flower choker and bracelet are made using wire and faceted beads and are finished with a flourish of velvet ribbon. The beaded flower pattern used to make this choker is relatively simple and once learned can be applied to making a huge array of jewellery. The bracelet uses the same pattern of beading for the flower but incorporates a larger vintage glass bead as a centre.

you will need

* 7 x 6mm faceted glass beads in brown (flower centres)

* 42 x 4mm faceted glass beads in pale pink (petals)

* 96 size 8 seed beads in amber

* 60in (153cm) length of 28 gauge beading wire (copper-coloured)

* 30in (76cm) of ¼in (6mm) wide velvet ribbon in chocolate brown

* Sewing thread in brown

making up instructions

NB: Refer to diagrams **A** to **F** on page 36.

Step 1
Take the beading wire and thread 12 seed beads onto the centre of the wire. Fold the wire loosely in half so that you have two working wires (**A**).

Step 2
Next take the tails of each wire and thread them in opposite directions through the hole of a 4mm pink faceted bead (**B**).

Step 3
On each tail, thread two 4mm pink faceted beads (**C**). Take both tails of wire together in the same direction through the centre of a 6mm brown faceted bead (**D**). Turn the 6mm bead up the other way so that the wire tails are facing downwards and the bead sits in the centre of the 4mm pink faceted beads. Then take each wire tail back through the two 4mm pink faceted beads on each side (**E**). NB: From figure **E** the seed beads are not shown.

Step 4
Next take the tails of each wire and thread them in opposite directions through another 4mm pink faceted bead (**F**).

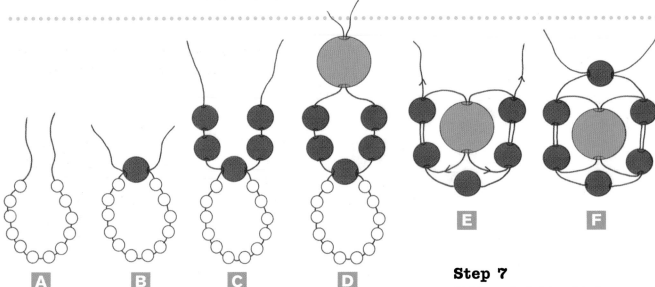

A   B   C   D   E   F

Step 5

Pick up six seed beads on each wire then take the tails of each wire and thread them in opposite directions through another 4mm pink faceted bead. You are now back to stage **B** and you should proceed with this pattern until you have made seven flowers.

Step 6

After the seventh flower, thread six seed beads on each wire tail, then take the tails through the beads on the opposite wire to form a loop. Continue working the wires back through beads in the opposite direction if the holes are open enough. If not, wrap the wire tails around the supporting wires between beads, clip the wire (being careful not to snip the supporting wire) and hide tails inside a bead (see **Working with Fine Gauge Wire**, page 22).

Step 7

Cut the velvet ribbon into two lengths of 15in (38cm). At one end of the choker fold one end of the ribbon around the bead loop, tucking under the raw edge and hand-stitch in place with small, neat stitches. Make a few stitches either side so that the ribbon cannot slip. Repeat on the other side of the choker.

Step 8

Cut the ends of the ribbon at an angle and put a dab of glue or Fray Check on to stop the ribbon

variations

This simple method for making a **wired flower** could be used with beads of most sizes, providing the centre bead is only proportionately larger than the petal beads to enable six petal beads to encircle it, without gaps.

Consider using one flower on an **earring** or making a larger flower as a feature for a wired or ribbon **choker**, or even a **brooch**. The **black choker** (pictured left) has been made using a large glass **bead** version of this flower to form the centre of an organdie ribbon bloom, created along the same lines as the flower in **Bessie** (page 44). The asymmetrically placed flower has beaded dangles to finish it off.

the matching bracelet

you will need

* 1 x 8mm brown faceted glass bead / antique bead
* 2 x 6mm brown faceted glass beads
* 6 x 6mm pink faceted glass beads
* 12 x 4mm pink faceted glass beads
* 48 size 8 seed beads
* 40in (102cm) of 28 gauge beading wire approx
* 6in (15cm) of ½in (6mm) velvet ribbon
* 2 small choker ends (for narrow ribbon)
* 5 jump rings
* 1 head pin
* 1 bolt ring fastener
* 1 each of seed bead, 4mm faceted and 6mm faceted beads for the dangle

You can make a bracelet the same way but with just three flowers, with the centre one larger than the other two. Follow the diagrams for the choker.

Step 1
Take the beading wire and thread 12 seed beads onto the centre of the wire. Fold the wire loosely in half so that you have two working wires (**A**).

Step 2
Next take the tails of each wire and thread them in opposite directions through a 4mm pink faceted bead (**B**). On each tail, thread two 4mm pink faceted beads (**C**).

Step 3
Take both tails of wire together in the same direction through the centre of a 6mm brown faceted bead (**D**). Turn the 6mm bead up the other way so that the wire tails are facing downwards and the beads sits in the centre of the 4mm pink faceted beads. Then take each wire tail back through the two 4mm pink faceted beads on each side (**E**). **NB: From figure E onwards the seed beads are not shown.**

Step 4
Next take the tails of each wire and thread them in opposite directions through another 4mm pink faceted bead (**F**).

Step 5
Pick up six seed beads on each wire then take the tails of each wire and thread them in opposite directions through a 6mm pink

bead. You are now back to step (**B**) but are using larger beads for the centre flower. Make the centre flower following the same figure but using the 6mm pink faceted beads as petals and the 8mm brown faceted bead as the centre.

Step 6
Thread another six seed beads onto each tail, make another flower using smaller beads to mirror the first, and then finish off as you did for the choker with a loop of 12 seed beads.

Step 7
Cut the ribbon into two lengths of 3in (8cm). Thread a length of ribbon through the bead loop at one end, folding it in half so that it is double and having raw ends even. Attach choker end using glue and pliers (refer to section on **Ribbon**, page 26). Repeat on other side. Attach bolt ring clasp to one end plate using a jump ring and at the other end attach the remaining four jump rings together in a chain.

Step 8
Make a dangle by threading a 6mm faceted, 4mm faceted and seed bead onto the head pin and turning a loop, following instructions for this in the section on **Making a Loop in Wire**, page 17. Attach dangle to bottom jump ring.

florence

ART NOUVEAU WIRE CHOKER WITH GLASS FLOWER

Art Nouveau jewellery designers featured flowers in their pieces that were not faithful copies of traditional blooms like roses – they were more often exotic or fantasy flowers set against the popular curving lines of the era.

This choker is stunning, partly because of its simplicity and because of the asymmetrically placed focal glass flower. It is a contemporary take on the Art Nouveau theme, but the twisted silver wires have a natural look and the pretty shimmering clear glass beads provide the perfect foil for the beautiful large glass bead flower.

To simplify the choker, you can make the flower without the central ring of small oval petals. You could also make the flower using plastic or wooden beads for a lightweight and more contemporary feel.

hints and tips

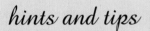

These materials and instructions should result in a choker which is approximately **15½in (40cm)** long and which sits fairly high in the neckline. Adding **jump rings** at the back (see page 13) allows for size variation.

You have two options for making the **central flower** for this choker. You can either make it up without the central ring of small oval petals by following only figures **A** to **D** in the diagrams, which is easier if you are not familiar with wire-working. If you want to make the **fuller flower** with the central ring of smaller oval petal beads, follow the instructions and refer to figures **A**, **B**, **C**, **E** and **F**.

For the whole project refer to the section on **Working with Fine Gauge Wire**, page 22.

you will need

* 140in (360cm) of 26 gauge wire cut into 2 lengths of 70in (180cm)

* 60in (153cm) of 26 or 28 gauge beading wire for the flower

* Approx 120 size 6 (or large) clear glass seed beads

* 6 large flat oval beads (approx 10 x 16mm)

* 1 size 8mm glass faceted bead for flower centre, preferably with large centre hole

* 6 small flat oval beads (optional for centre ring of petals – approx 6 x 8mm)

* 8 glass beads with large holes in the centre

* 7 large crimps

* Large lobster clasp

* 1 closed jump ring

* 4 to 6 open jump rings (depending on sizing required)

* Short head pin for dangle

* 1 small oval glass bead and 3 seed beads (or a similar assortment) for the dangle

making up instructions

Start by making the glass flower following the diagrams in figures **A** to **D** or **A** to **F** below, depending on which flower you are making.

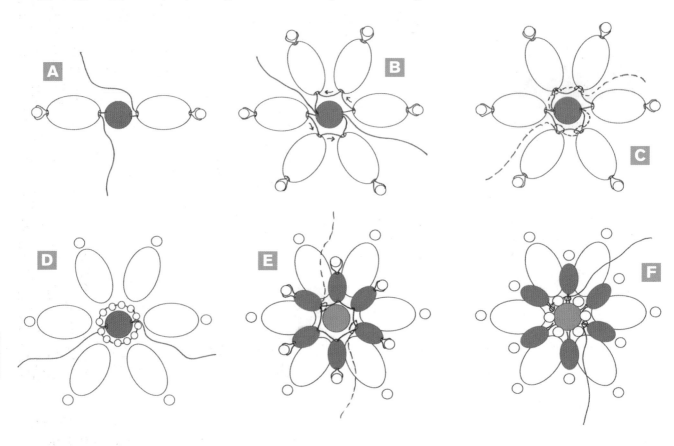

the flower

Step 1

Take the 60in (153cm) length of 28 or 26 gauge beading wire and thread on the large 8mm centre bead to the centre of the wire. On one tail, thread on a flat oval bead, a seed bead then take the wire back through the oval bead and pull the wire up tight. Push the centre bead against this.

Step 2

On the other wire tail, thread on another flat oval bead, a seed bead and take the wire back through the oval bead. Push the oval bead up against the centre bead and pull the wires tight so that both petals are sitting flush up against the centre bead, one on either side (**A**).

Step 3

With one wire tail pick up another flat oval bead, seed bead and take the wire back through the oval bead. Push the oval bead so that it is sitting next to the previous petal, then pull the wire tight. Thread on another petal in the same way so that there are three petals on this side. Take the tail of this wire back through the large centre bead in a circle and pull up tight.

Repeat with the wire on the opposite side of the flower (so that there are three petals on this wire also) then take the wire tail through the centre bead in a circle (in the opposite direction to the first wire) and pull up tight (**B**).

Step 4

To stabilize the petals, take one of the wire tails and guide it under the stem of the petal next to it and wrap it around the stem once, then move onto the next two stems. Do the same with the wire tail and three petals on the other side and finish up with the two wires at opposite sides of the flower (**C**).

Step 5

On one wire, thread enough seed beads to encircle half of the central bead. This could be anything from six to 12 seed beads depending on their size. Next take the wire back through the centre bead in a circle. Repeat this with the other tail, then take the tail through the centre bead in the opposite direction to the first. You are now at step (**D**).

At this point you can finish off the flower by taking the wires under the oval petal stems and wrapping them around the stems a few times. Finally thread the wires through an adjacent bead if possible and cut off tails, hiding any sharp ends inside beads if possible. (Refer to section on **Working with Fine Gauge Wire**, page 22.)

Step 6

If you wish to add the centre ring of small oval petals, do this after you have stabilized the first ring of large oval petals at **C**. The wires should now be between petals on opposite sides of the flower. To continue, on one of the wires thread on a small oval bead, seed

bead and go back through the small oval bead, then take the wire down under the stem of the large petal, wrap it around once, then come up in between the next two large petals. Add two more small petals with this wire and then repeat with wire on the opposite side (**E**).

Step 7

Finally add a large size 6 or 8 seed bead in the same way in between each small oval petal and by wrapping the wire around the supporting stem of each small petal you have just attached (**F**). Thread the wires through an adjacent bead if possible and cut off tails, hiding any sharp ends

inside beads if possible. (Refer to section on **Working with Fine Gauge Wire**, page 22.)

variations

This large glass bead flower is suitable for stitching onto **ribbon cuffs** or **chokers** and could be wired to a brooch backing bar, flanked with silk or velvet **leaves** as a **brooch**.

the choker

NB: Refer to figures (A) to (D) in Rosaline, page 93, for help.

Step 1
Start by taking both of the 70in (180cm) wires together through the hole in the lobster clasp. Find the centre of the wires and fold the wires in half over the clasp so that you have four equal length pieces of wire to work with. Then thread all four wires through one large-holed bead and a large crimp.

Push the bead and crimp up fairly tight against the clasp and squash the crimp, taking care not to sever any wires.

Step 2
Work all four strands at the same time. Begin by threading two seed beads onto the first wire. Take the wire around the beads and back through the holes again in a circle (in the same direction), thus securing them in place. On the first strand, thread a total of around five beads. You can leave some of the beads 'loose' without securing them in place to achieve movement and random effect and you can secure some beads singly. Repeat this step for all four strands.

Step 3
Next thread all four wires through a large-holed bead and large crimp and another large-holed bead. Push the beads/crimp up towards

▼ This choker takes on a totally different appearance when made in a solid colour.

the beads you have threaded on and when you are satisfied with the arrangement, squash the crimp in place with pliers. The first bead and crimp block should be 2½–3in (6–8cm) from the end bead/crimp. Fan out the four wires to form a 'scallop' effect.

Step 4

For the next section, thread/secure five seed beads onto each strand as before. Take all wires through another large-holed bead, large crimp and large-holed bead. Again this bead and crimp block should be around 2½–3in (6–8cm) from the last block. When you are satisfied with the arrangement, squash the crimp in place.

Step 5

Thread seed beads on for another scallop, then thread on a large crimp only and squash it in place. Fan out the wires, then taking the top wire of the four, attach to the top of the flower you have made. Do this by winding the wire around the supporting stems of the large petals at the top of the flower. Take the bottom of the four wires and attach to the bottom of the flower by winding the wire around the supporting stems of the large petals at the bottom of the flower. Wind the wire around each stem twice.

Step 6

Make sure the flower is stable, then with the two centre wires lying across the back of the flower centre bead, take all four wires through another large crimp, push

hints and tips

Take care not to overwork or over twist the wire – if it breaks it cannot be replaced easily especially where it is exposed.

the crimp up tight against the flower, and then squash in place.

Step 7

Make another scallop, thread on another large-holed bead/large crimp/large-holed bead block, and then make a final (fifth) scallop.

Step 8

Next thread all four wires through a large crimp, large glass bead and a closed jump ring. Take the wires back through the bead and the crimp. Push them so that they are about 2½–3in (6–8cm) from the previous large-holed bead/large crimp block.

Step 9

Pull the wire strands up tight to form a loop over the jump ring (you may have to do this one strand at a time and you definitely have to take great care) and push the bead and crimp tight up against it.

Step 10

Squash the crimp, and then wrap the tails of the wire around the crimp and supporting wires several times. Cut off the tails of two strands and wrap the remaining two strands around several times to cover the ends (see **Finishing Off with Fine Wire**, page 23).

Step 11

Clip the final tails and hide up against the bead.

Step 12

Add another jump ring to the closed ring. This will be used to fasten the choker. If you want to make it multi-sized, you can add several jump rings in a chain and attach a dangle to the bottom ring. Make the dangle by threading a small oval bead and two seed beads onto a head pin and turning a loop at the top (see **Making a Loop in Wire**, page 17).

Step 13

Finish off the choker by 'twisting' the wire in between the seed beads. Do this by grasping the wire with round nose pliers and twisting the pliers in a clockwise direction, thus twisting the wire in an 'S' shape. Hold the pliers with the points downward and support the wires in the palm of your hand. Twist the wire once or twice on each strand in each scallop in a random manner between beads. **NB: Twisting the wire in this way will lose around 2in (5cm) from the overall length of the choker.**

bessie

ART NOUVEAU CORSAGE (ROUNDED-PETAL
RIBBON FLOWER)

Corsages have made a huge fashion comeback in the last
decade. Beautiful textile blooms currently adorn everything from
cardigans to handbags. In Victorian times, flowers and cockades
were fashioned from ribbon to embellish hats, belts and frocks.

This project uses ribbon petals on a felt base, flanked with velvet leaves and finished with a velvet-covered button centre with vintage sequins. The flower would look wonderful on the lapel of a tweed jacket or possibly on a chunky knit or tweedy handbag. The applications for this type of flower are limitless – it could be made from organdie ribbon to adorn a delicate cuff for example.

you will need

* 15in (38cm) of velvet ribbon, 1½in (38mm) wide for petals

* Piece of felt 4½ x 2½in (11.5 x 6.5cm) for base

* Piece of buckram 2in square (5cm square) for base

* Brooch backing bar (with holes for stitching)

* Cover button – size 1¼in (3cm) diameter for centre

* Piece of velvet 2½in square (6.5cm square) to cover button

* 8 sequins (vintage or modern)

* 8 seed beads

* Group of 3 purchased velvet or silk leaves on wire stems

making up instructions

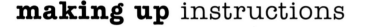

Step 1

First make a base for the corsage. Using the circular pattern templates below cut out two corsage base pieces from felt and one corsage base buckram piece from buckram.

Step 2

Place the buckram circle centrally in between the two felt circles. Pin in the centre, then using a short machine stitch, sew circles together round the outside edge, about ¼in (6mm) from the outside edge. (Throughout this project refer to section on **Corsages and Other Textile Projects**, page 30.)

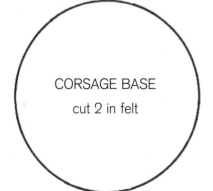

CORSAGE BASE
cut 2 in felt

CORSAGE BASE
BUCKRAM PIECE
cut 1

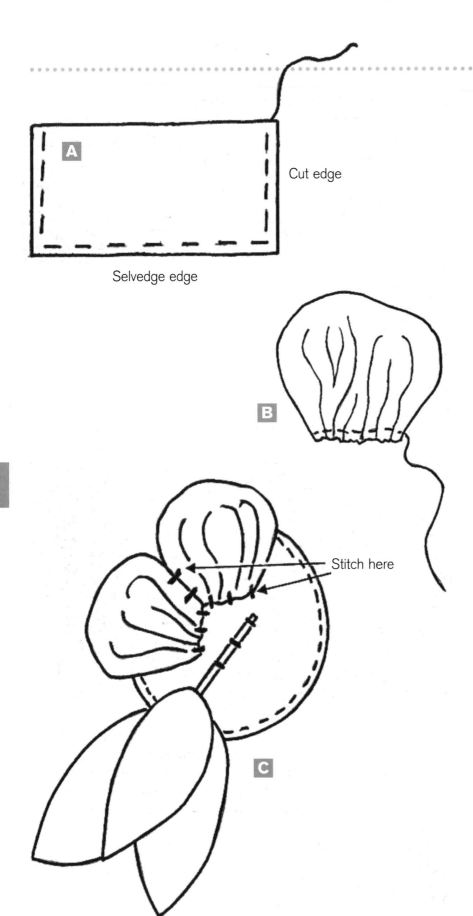

Cut edge

Selvedge edge

Stitch here

You can make this flower
using any width of ribbon
you like, from 1in (25mm)
wide. You can use velvet,
satin or organdie ribbon –
each has different
properties and looks very
different when finished.
For each 'Round-petal
Flower', you will need a
length of ribbon which is
10 times the width
measurement.

Step 3

For each petal, cut a piece of
ribbon with a length twice as long
as the width. This project uses
1½in (38mm) wide ribbon so you
will need to cut a piece 3in
(7.5cm) in length for each petal.
You will need five lengths/petals
for this flower.

Step 4

For each individual petal run a
continuous gathering stitch along
one cut edge, one selvedge edge
and the other cut edge (**A**). With
velvet ribbon, ensure that you are
using the ribbon the same way up
for each petal.

Step 5

Pull gathering stitches up tightly to
form a rounded-shaped petal (**B**).
All of the gathers will now be at
the base of the petal.

Secure the gathers with a few
stitches at one side, then go back

through the gathers again and secure at the other side. Make five petals in this way.

Step 6

You can now stitch the petals directly onto the felt corsage base. Stitch your purchased leaves to the base first with the wire in the centre so that it will be covered by the petals/centre. Stitch leaves to the base over the wire stems in three places (**C**).

Step 7

Arrange petals around the outside of the base in a flower shape. The side edges of the petals will meet, they will overlap the outside edge of the base by around ½in (13mm) and there will be a space in the middle of the petals about 1in (25mm) in diameter. Hand-stitch the petals in place, at the bottom (gathered) edge of each petal to the felt base and at the side edges of each petal to each other, see step (**C**).

Step 8

Make a 'centre' for your flower. The centre of this flower was made using a covered button 1¼in (approx 30mm) in size. First cut out a circle of velvet or silk to adequately cover your button (allowing tuck room). Stitch a cluster of sequins onto the centre of this fabric circle. Thread a needle with a double length of matching thread. Make a knot in the thread and secure on the reverse of the circle with a few stitches. Bring the needle and

thread up through the sequin and a seed bead, and then take the needle back down through the sequin. The seed bead will keep the sequin in place. You may wish to repeat the sequence for extra security. Attach eight sequins in this manner, and then cover the button with the fabric/sequin circle following manufacturer's guidelines.

Step 9

Stitch the button in the centre of the flower. This will cover the raw lower edges of the petals.

Step 10

Finally, stitch a brooch bar on to the back of the corsage base, at the centre top so that the corsage will not hang down when pinned onto clothing.

variations

The **cuff** pictured above is made using the same flower. The cuff base is made from **velvet ribbon** backed with **grosgrain ribbon** and finished with **metal end plates** like the choker in **Loretta** (page 52). The flower petals are made from 1in (25mm) **organdie ribbon** and the **button** in the centre is covered in silk with a cluster of matching **seed beads**. A fluffy **feather** finishes off the piece.

making **vintage** jewellery

you will need

* 13in (33cm) of velvet ribbon ⅝in (16mm) wide

* 13in (33cm) of satin or grosgrain ribbon for backing, same width or slightly narrower than the velvet ribbon

* 1 purchased or made ribbon rose approx ¾in (19mm) in size

* 10 x 4mm beads in amethyst

* 17 x 4mm beads in black

* 18 seed beads, size 8 in black

* Long feathers (approx 8) (coloured emu feathers were used in this project)

* 36in (92cm) of 28 gauge non-tarnish beading wire

* 2 choker end plates (to fit width of ribbon)

* Small lobster or bolt ring fastener

* 9 small jump rings

* 1 short head pin

loretta

FLOWER AND FEATHER CHOKER WITH MATCHING PURSE BAG

In the 1910s feather plumes were often used to adorn fashion accessories. Chokers were also very fashionable in this era and velvet bands or silk ribbons often formed the basis for these popular accessories.

Loretta combines lots of different textures and uses velvet ribbon, long feathers and facetted beads to produce a stunning choker. The off-centre focal decoration from the choker has also been used to trim a slim velvet evening purse, made with a matching beaded handle. Make just one or use the two pieces together for party or evening wear with a touch of 1910s decadence and glamour.

making up instructions

Step 1
Stitch the ribbon backing to the velvet ribbon down both edges using a short machine stitch. Iron from the reverse side to even out any puckers.

Step 2
Add glue to each end of the ribbon and attach end plates (refer to **Ribbon and Textiles**, page 26).

Step 3
Join eight jump rings together in a chain and attach to one end plate. Make a 'dangle' for the back by threading one seed bead, one amethyst 4mm, one black 4mm, another amethyst 4mm and a final seed bead. Turn a loop at the top (refer to **Making a Loop in Wire**, page 17). Attach to end jump ring in

the chain. At the other end of the choker join the clasp to the end plate using the remaining jump ring.

Step 4
Make the beaded backing for the flower. Take the piece of beading wire and at one end thread on two black 4mm beads, one seed bead, one amethyst 4mm bead, one seed bead and another black 4mm bead. Push the beads to about 6in (15cm) from the end of the wire. Then take the long end of the wire back through the first 4mm black bead in an anti-clockwise direction to form a circle of beads (**A**). The long end (working end) of the wire will be coming out of the bead to the right and the short 6in (15cm) tail will be coming out of the bead facing the left.

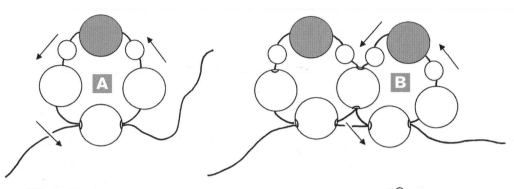

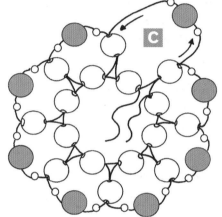

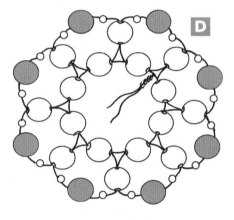

Step 5

Now pick up two 4mm black beads, one seed bead, one amethyst 4mm bead and one seed bead. Take the working wire down through the black 4mm bead on the right of the previous circle and through the first 4mm bead you added in the new circle (**B**). You must continue to pick up the same sequence of beads and follow the same step as above until you have threaded on seven of the amethyst 4mm beads.

Step 6

After bringing the working wire out of the last black 4mm horizontal bead in the circle, add a 4mm black bead then take the wire upwards, following the same anti-clockwise direction, through the left-hand side vertical bead from the first circle you made. Add one seed bead, one amethyst 4mm bead, one seed bead, then take the wire down through the last black vertical 4mm bead next to it (on its left) (**C**). Bring the wire back through the bottom horizontal black 4mm bead so that both tails of wire are now next to each other.

Twist the wires together a few times (**D**), then if you can, take the tails back through a few beads, clip the tails and hide them inside the beads. Take care not to clip the supporting wire. (For more tips refer to **Working with Fine Gauge Wire**, page 22.)

Step 7

Hand-stitch the ribbon rose into the centre of the beaded backing. Place the rose on top of the beaded backing so that it sits in the central hole. Hand-stitch in place from the back by stitching round the supporting wire in between each of the bottom/inside row of 4mm beads.

Gather the feathers together and tie together. Take the thread around the bunch a few times and tie again. Trim the quill ends back and stitch the bunch to the choker approximately 4½in (11.5cm) from the choker end on the right-hand side as it is laying flat, right side up, in front of you.

Step 8

Finally, stitch the flower/bead feature centrally over the top of the feather quills. Stitch around the supporting wire at the base of each vertical 4mm black bead in the circle.

the matching purse bag

dimensions

The finished bag measures 10 (at longest length) x 5¼in (25 x 13.5cm), excluding the handle

templates

page 150

suggested fabrics

for main bag fabric:
short-pile cotton velveteen or firm silk

for bag lining:
quilted cotton or satin

you will need

* Piece of short-pile cotton velveteen 26in (66cm) wide by 9in (23cm) deep

* Piece of medium/firm iron-on interfacing 26in (66cm) wide by 9in (23cm) deep

* Piece of quilted lining fabric 26in (66cm) wide by 9in (23cm) deep

* 8in (20cm) zipper

* Piece of ⅝in (16mm) width velvet ribbon, 10in (25cm) long for trim

For the handle

* 11 x 6mm black glass faceted beads

* 22 x 4mm amethyst glass faceted beads

* Approx 75 size 8 black seed beads

* Piece of tiger tail beading wire 22in (56cm) long

* 2 large crimp beads

For the trim

* 1 purchased or made ribbon rose approx ¾in (19mm) in size

* 8 x 4mm beads in amethyst

* 16 x 4mm beads in black

* 16 seed beads, size 8 in black

* Long feathers, approx 8 (coloured emu feathers used in this project)

* 36in (92cm) of 28 gauge non-tarnish beading wire

cutting out

* Cut two pieces on fold from velvet fabric

* Cut two pieces on fold from iron-on medium/heavy interfacing

* Cut two pieces on fold from lining fabric

hints and tips

You will need to use the pattern template on page 150, which is full size, but is drawn on the fold. This means you will have to cut the pieces on the fold of the fabric.

making up instructions

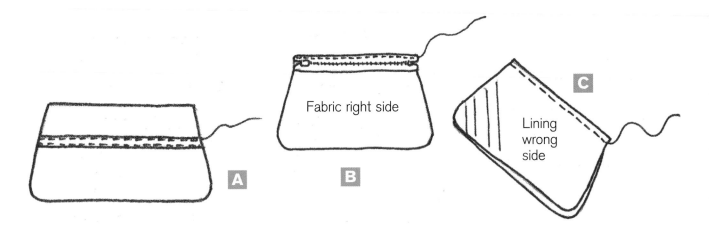

Fabric right side

Lining wrong side

A B C

Step 1

Iron interfacing onto wrong side of each purse main fabric section.

Step 2

Stitch the ribbon trim to the purse in the position shown on the pattern template down both outside edges using a short machine stitch (**A**).

Step 3

Whipstitch the open end of the zipper tape together.

Step 4

Make the handle loop by ironing the fusible web to the wrong side of handle loop piece, peeling off the paper backing and folding long edges (marked with dotted line on pattern piece) into the centre and fusing in place. Fold loop in half so that raw edges are even and baste stitch together about ½in (13mm) from the raw edges. Stitch onto purse front on left-hand side at position marked on pattern piece. Stitch over basting.

Step 5

Pin the zipper to upper edge of one purse piece then using a zipper foot, stitch approximately ⅛in (3mm) from the teeth of the zipper (**B**).

Step 6

Pin one lining piece to the upper edge of the purse, having right sides together and raw edges even. Stitch over previous line of stitching. The zipper will be sandwiched in between (**C**).

Step 7

Turn right side out and press both lining and fabric away from zipper (**D**).

Step 8

Complete the other side of the purse in the same way (**E**).

Step 9

Open the zipper three-quarters of the way. Place right sides of purse and lining together as in diagram **F**. Stitch around outside edge of purse, up to zipper on each side. Stitch lining up to zipper each side,

leaving a gap of around 4in (10cm) in base of lining for turning the purse through. Stitch with a ½in (13mm) seam allowance. Note that the handle loop will be sandwiched in the seam.

Step 10

Turn purse right side out, slip-stitch the gap in the lining and push lining to inside of purse. Close zipper and press thoroughly through a cloth.

Step 11

After you have turned the purse right side out, you will need to hand-stitch a few stitches on the outside of the purse at either end of the zipper tape to keep the zipper ends held together and tucked in neatly.

Step 12

Make the beaded handle for the purse. Take the length of tiger tail beading wire and thread on a pattern of 1 x 4mm amethyst glass bead, 1 x size 8 seed bead, 1 x 4mm amethyst glass bead, 2 x size 8 seed beads, 1 x 6mm

Fabric right side

D

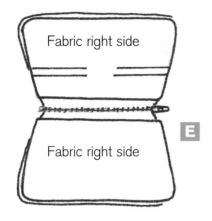

Fabric right side

Fabric right side

E

Fabric wrong side

Lining wrong side

F

black glass bead and two size 8 seed beads. Repeat this until you have threaded on 10 black 6mm glass beads, then after the final two seed beads, finish with a 4mm amethyst glass bead, seed bead and another 4mm amethyst glass bead.

Step 13

Next take both wire tails through a large crimp bead, 6mm glass black bead and another large crimp bead. On one wire tail thread 20 size 8 seed beads and then thread through the handle loop on the purse. Thread the other wire through the seed beads in the opposite direction, and then take both wire tails back up through the crimp beads and 6mm black bead. Separate the two wires and take each one back up through a few of the previous beads. Pull the wires up so that the beads are snug together without making the handle too stiff. When happy with the arrangement, squash the crimp beads securely and trim the wire tails. (See **Madeline**, page 80, for further help.)

Step 14

Bundle feathers together, as in step 8, of the choker instructions. Stitch to the bag with the feather ends facing downwards and the quills centered on the ribbon approximately 2½in (6cm) from the right front seam.

Step 15

Make beaded backing for the ribbon flower as in choker instructions and stitch to purse around the supporting wires over the feather quills.

variations

For both the choker and the purse bag **shorter** fluffy feathers can be used if you cannot find long feathers. You could also substitute the **ribbon flower** for a **vintage glass button** in the centre of the bead surround. You could also add a few long **silk ribbons** to the feathers for texture.

eva

1910s TRELLIS CLUSTER EARRINGS

Although influenced by the art nouveau styles of the 1910s, these earrings are very much in keeping with the current trend for 'dangly' or chandelier earrings. The wire framework provides the ideal base from which to suspend different jewelled objects and beads.

The basic shape of these earrings is made using a wire jig with a pretty wrapped loop at the top. There are contrasting variations for the decorative dangles. The pink and silver cluster earrings have a more delicate appearance while the copper glass leaf pair has more of the art nouveau styling. The cluster can also be used to create a simpler but striking pair of earrings on a straight head pin.

you will need

* 20in (approx 50cm) of 18 or 20 gauge silver-plated hobby wire, 10 inches (approx 25cm) for each earring

* 1 pair of silver ear wires

* 4 short silver head pins

* 4 x 3mm silver ball beads

* 2 jump rings

* 24in (60cm) of 28 gauge silver-coloured beading wire (12in (30cm) to make each cluster)

* 28 size 4mm semi-precious stone beads (rose quartz)

making up instructions

Step 1

Cut the 18/20 gauge wire into two lengths of 10in (25cm). You should make one earring framework at a time. Begin by making a loop at one end of one piece of wire using round nose pliers. **NB: The loop must be large enough to fit over the pegs in the wire jig.** Place the pegs in the wire jig in the pattern (**A**).

Step 2

Place the loop of the wire over the top peg in the pattern, with the loop facing to the left. Then wind the wire under the next peg and around it in an anti-clockwise direction. Move onto the next peg and do the same (**B**). Remember as you wind to push the wire down with your finger, a file or a piece of dowelling.

Step 3

Next take the wire down over the top and to the left of the bottom peg in the pattern. Wind it around the peg in an anti-clockwise direction, then take the peg up to the next peg (**C**).

Step 4

Complete the wrapping and take the wire over the top and to the right (**D**).

Step 5

Gently remove the framework from the jig and grasp the wire tail and wrap it around the 'stem' of the earring two to three times, finishing under the loop (**E**). For this also refer to **Wrapped Loops**, page 21. Cut the wire at the back of the earring using wire cutters.

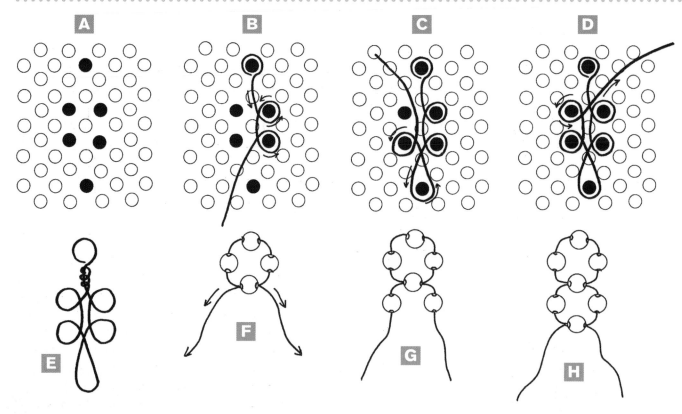

Step 6

You must now 'reshape' the earring using a soft cloth and pliers to flatten it into the desired shape (refer to **General Techniques for Using a Wire Jig**, page 20).

Step 7

Make a second earring framework. You can do this while the first is still on the jig if you like. Wind the wire in the opposite direction if you feel confident enough to make the second earring a 'mirror image' of the first.

Step 8

Attach an earring wire to the top loop of each earring framework by opening and closing the loop on the earring wire as you would a jump ring.

Step 9

Make two dangles for each earring by threading a 4mm stone bead and a silver ball bead onto each of the four head pins and turning a loop at the top (refer to section on **Making a Loop in Wire**, page 17). Attach these to the lower side loops of each framework. Remember to form the loop completely first then open/close it as you would a jump ring.

Step 10

Make a bead 'cluster' for each earring by following steps (**F**) to (**J**). Thread three 4mm stone beads onto the centre of a 12in (30cm) length of 28 gauge beading wire. Then take both wire tails in opposite directions through the centre of a fourth 4mm stone bead to form a circle (**J**).

Step 11

Pick up another 4mm stone bead on each wire tail (**G**) then cross the tails in opposite directions through another 4mm stone bead (**H**). Repeat this again then add another 4mm stone bead onto each tail (**I**).

Step 12

Take both wire tails and thread them in opposite directions through the very first centre bead threaded at the other end (**J**). Pull the wires up tight to form a beaded ball or cluster. If the holes in the beads are large enough, thread the wires back through adjacent beads, wrap the wires around the supporting wires on each side, then clip the tails and hide them inside a bead if possible (refer to **Finishing Off with Fine Wire**, page 23).

making **vintage** jewellery

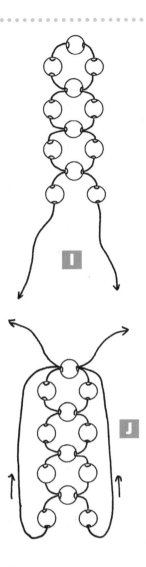

I

J

Step 13

Attach a jump ring between beads around a supporting wire where convenient and while the jump ring is open attach the cluster to the bottom loop in the earring framework with the ring.

Step 14

Finally, reshape the earring a little with pliers if necessary to ensure that all dangles hang correctly.

To make the **trellis leaf** version of the earrings (pictured below left) use the same amount of wire and make the same basic framework following steps (**A**) to (**E**). Then make two **dangles** for each earring by threading a seed bead, a 4mm faceted glass bead and another seed bead onto each of the four head pins and turning a loop at the top. Attach these to the lower side loops of each framework. On the bottom loop of each framework hang a **glass leaf** bead.

The **chocolate**-coloured pair of earrings (below) uses 'clusters' of small 4mm glass pearls, made following steps **F** to **J**. Then for each earring on a long head pin thread a 4mm bead, seed bead, a teardrop-shaped bead and a 4mm bead. Then thread on the cluster, pushing it down so that the last 4mm bead is inside it. Next, thread on a 6mm bead, seed bead, 4mm bead and a final seed bead, and then turn a loop at the top. Finally, attach to an earring wire. These are simple to make and could be fashioned from any combination of beads for a variety of vintage looks.

1920s

clarissa

LONG SAUTOIR NECKLACE

This unusual necklace has the slightly longer length characteristic of styles of the 1920s. The 'horseshoe' shape is also reminiscent of the embroidered décolletage of dresses of this period.

Clarissa has clean fluid lines and works best made up in neutral colours like rich chocolate browns, blacks and greys. It would be easy to imagine this necklace being worn with a 1920s flapper dress. It takes a little time to ensure that the front section of the necklace hangs correctly but it is quite easily mastered and will make a stunning decoration for a simple evening frock or boat-neck top.

making up instructions

Step 1
Start in the middle of the necklace. Make the 'dangle' first using one of the headpins. Thread on one teardrop bead, one seed bead, the large flat oval glass bead and two seed beads. Turn a loop at the top of the beads making sure that the loop is properly closed (refer to **Making a Loop in Wire**, page 17).

Step 2
Thread the dangle onto the centre of one of the lengths of tiger tail. Thread two 6mm glass beads, one teardrop bead and two 6mm glass beads each side of the dangle.

Step 3
Take each end of the tiger tail through the outside holes of the spacer bar, leaving the centre hole empty (**A**). Add two 6mm glass beads on each side (above the

space bar), then a crimp bead. At this point it is vital to arrange beads so that the 'dangle' hangs correctly – not too tight or stiff. Once happy with the arrangement squash the crimp beads securing the 'horseshoe' shape at the bottom of the necklace in place (**B**).

Step 4
Make the centre head pin next. As well as being a decorative part of the design, this pin will help to stabilize the necklace. Thread a seed bead then a 6mm glass bead onto the head pin. Thread the head pin through the middle hole in the space bar pointing upwards. Then thread on a teardrop bead, two 3mm gold balls and a 6mm glass bead. Turn a loop at the top ensuring that the loop is properly closed (refer to **Making a Loop in Wire**, page 17) (**C**).

you will need

* 60in (approx 153cm) of tigertail wire, cut into 2 lengths of approx 30in (76cm)
* Approx 160 size 8 seed beads (with central holes big enough to take 2 strands of tiger tail)
* 30 x 3mm gold-coloured balls
* 8 teardrop-shaped glass pearl beads (size approx 10 x 6mm)
* 28 x 6mm round brown glass beads
* 1 large flat oval glass bead (approx 15 x 12mm) or other feature bead
* 6 small flat oval glass beads (approx 8 x 6mm)
* 2 long head pins
* 1 x 3-hole spacer bar
* 2 calottes
* 6–8 crimps
* 1 barrel fastener
* 2 jump rings

making **vintage** jewellery

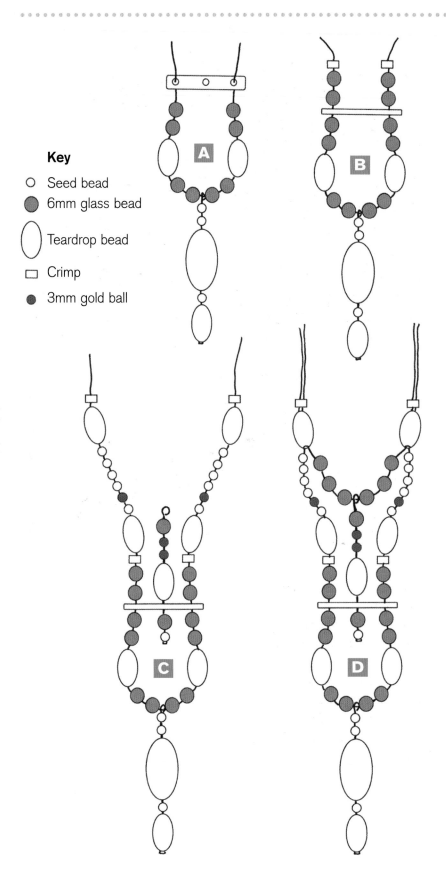

Key

○ Seed bead

● 6mm glass bead

○ Teardrop bead

▢ Crimp

● 3mm gold ball

Step 5

Now on each side of the first tiger tail strand after the crimp, add a teardrop bead, a seed bead, a 3mm gold ball, four seed beads, another teardrop bead and a crimp.

Step 6

Now take the second strand of tiger tail through the loop of the upward pointing head pin. Add three 6mm glass beads each side, then take each end of the second tiger tail strand through the last teardrop bead and the crimp threaded on the first strand, each side. **NB: It is vital at this point to adjust the beads to hang correctly.** Do not pull the strands up too tightly – there should be a ¼in (6mm) gap either side of the 6mm glass beads on the second strand and the shared teardrop bead so that the four seed beads on either side can sit correctly (**D**). Only when you are happy with the arrangement crimp both wires together in place. Don't crimp until you are certain that your front centrepiece hangs right! From now on you will thread beads onto both strands together, treating them as one.

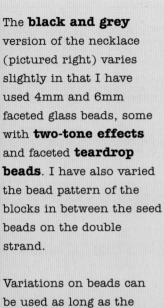
The **black and grey** version of the necklace (pictured right) varies slightly in that I have used 4mm and 6mm faceted glass beads, some with **two-tone effects** and faceted **teardrop beads**. I have also varied the bead pattern of the blocks in between the seed beads on the double strand.

Variations on beads can be used as long as the 'spacing' and bead size for the **horseshoe-shaped front section** remains the same – this will ensure that the necklace hangs correctly when it is worn.

Step 7

Add one 6mm glass bead each side, one 3mm gold ball, then 12 seed beads. Next add one 3mm gold ball, one small glass oval bead and one 3mm gold ball. Add another 12 seed beads. Add another 3mm gold ball, 6mm glass bead and 3mm gold ball followed by 12 seed beads. Follow the stringing pattern of adding 12 seed beads until you have six blocks of 12 seed beads each side with alternating 6mm and small oval beads in between the blocks. Finish with a 3mm gold ball, 6mm glass bead and 3mm gold ball block. Attach calottes with remaining crimps and add barrel fastener with jump rings (refer to **Using End Findings**, page 16).

freida

1920s CONTEMPORARY TASSEL NECKLACE AND MATCHING EARRINGS

Tassels were a prominent feature of 1920s jewellery and fashions. This necklace and earrings set uses flexible tiger tail beading wire and sparsely placed crimped beads to create a contemporary take on the traditional beaded thread tassels.

The necklace can be made using any combination of smaller beads, lozenge or disc-shaped beads. It is ideal for showing off an unusual or large feature bead as a centrepiece.

Ensure that the central hole of the feature bead is large enough for six strands of tiger tail wire. The earrings can be made to match the necklace or can make a statement in their own right.

making up instructions

Step 1

Take the three 10in (25cm) strands of tiger tail and feed the three ends together through the centre of the large feature bead in an upwards direction (**A**). Fold the ends over loosely at the centre point of the wires and take them back down through the feature bead. You will now have a loop of wires at the top of the feature bead and six tails coming out of the bottom of the feature bead (**B**).

Step 2

Take the two 20in (50cm) strands of tiger tail together and thread them through the loop of wires above the feature bead (**C**). Position the loop in the centre of the two wires and gradually pull the six short tails, thus pulling the loop tighter.

Step 3

Thread all six short tails through the large crimp. Make sure that the tails are sitting correctly and that you have left enough 'hanging' space in the loop, then squash the crimp flat to secure the tassel in place (**D**).

Step 4

On either side of the tassel, threading on both wires together, thread one silver ball, one 6mm bead, two size 8 seeds, one 6mm bead, one silver ball and a crimp. Ensure that the tassel is hanging correctly then squash the crimp either side to secure the front section in place (**E**).

Step 5

On one main strand only, approximately 1¼in (3cm) above the last front section bead, thread

you will need

* 70in (approx 180cm) of tiger tail wire cut into 2 lengths of 20in (50cm) for the main necklace and 3 lengths of 10in (25cm) for the tassel

* 1 large feature bead with a centre hole large enough to take 6 strands of tiger tail wire

* 1 large crimp

* Approximately 24 small crimps

* 2 clam shell calottes

* 2–3 jump rings

* Fastener of your choice

* 17 or 18 black size 4mm beads

* 7 or 8 black size 6mm beads

* 18 red size 8 seed beads

* Approximately 22 x 3mm silver-coloured balls

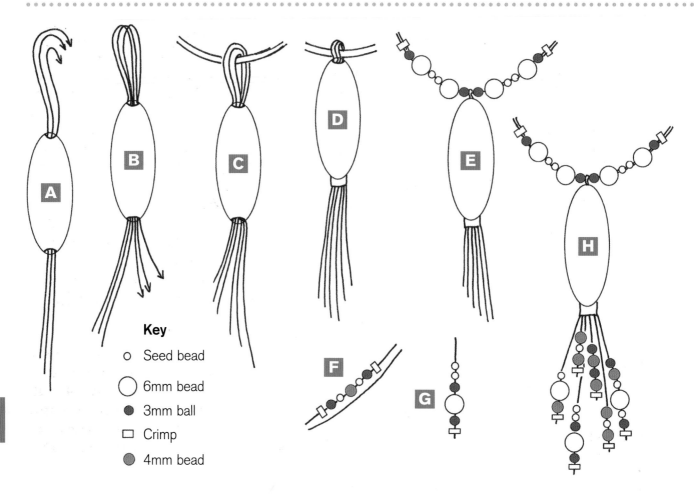

Key

o   Seed bead

◯   6mm bead

●   3mm ball

▢   Crimp

●   4mm bead

on a crimp and squash in place. Then thread on one silver ball, one size 8 seed, one 4mm bead, one size 8 seed, one silver ball, then another crimp. Squash in place to secure (**F**). Repeat on other side.

Step 6

Approximately 2½in (6cm) above this on the same strand, squash another crimp and thread one 4mm bead, one silver ball and one 4mm bead, then squash another crimp to secure.

Step 7

On the other strand, approximately 2¾in (7cm) above the last front section bead, squash a crimp, then thread one silver ball, one 4mm bead, one size 8 seed, one 4mm bead, one silver ball, then squash another crimp to secure.

Step 8

Thread a calotte and a crimp onto both wires at one end. Squash crimp (crimping both wires together) where you want the end to be (this will be approx 2in (5cm) above the last bead block), trim back tails and close the calotte over the crimp. Repeat on the other side of the necklace and attach the catch to the end with the jump rings (refer to section on **Using End Findings**, page 16).

Step 9

To complete the tassel, take one strand at a time. Thread a mixture of beads onto each strand (for example, an 8mm seed, one 6mm bead and one silver ball) and squash a crimp where you want the end of the tassel to hang. Cut back the tail to the crimp (**G**). This necklace looks best if the strands of the tassel are all different lengths, so it is worth taking time with placing the crimps and mixing the beads (**H**). (You could have the same bead pattern on two strands, so that you have three pairs.)

to make the matching earrings

you will need

* 16in (41cm) of tiger tail wire (8in (20cm) approx for each earring)
* 10 crimps
* 10 size 8 seed beads
* 12 x 3mm silver balls
* 2 small red oval beads
* 2 small black oval beads
* 2 small red rectangle beads
* 2 earring posts/wires

Step 1
Cut two lengths of tiger tail – one of 5½in (14cm) and one of 2½in (6cm) for each earring.

Step 2
Make a crease in one 5½in (14cm) wire at a point where the ends will be uneven. Do the same for the other earring making sure that they are a 'pair'.

Step 3
Thread the end of the creased wire through the earring wire loop (make sure that the gap in the loop is completely closed so that the wire cannot escape) so that the crease is central around the loop (**A**).

Step 4
Thread the two tails through a crimp, then push the tail of the 2½in (6cm) wire up through the crimp also. Squash the crimp

making sure that you have left enough 'hanging' space at the top and that the extra wire is secured (**B**). You can clip any excess wire from above the crimp if necessary, but be careful not to cut the loop over the ear wire. You now have three strands per earring.

Step 5
Next thread a size 8 seed bead, a 3mm silver ball and a crimp onto all three wires together and push them up against the first crimp. Squash the second crimp (**C**).

Step 6
Thread a selection of beads and a crimp onto each tail and squash the crimp where you want the last bead to hang, then clip the excess wire tail. Make sure that the three tails are uneven. Make sure that you make a pair!

hints and tips

The basic instructions and techniques for the earrings can be used with any mix of beads from antique facetted beads with aged finish findings to vintage glass flowers with coloured tiger tail. As so few are needed you can also use up leftover beads.

Key
- ⬭ Seed bead
- ▭ Crimp
- ⬤ 3mm ball
- ⬬ Small oval bead
- ▯ Rectangle bead

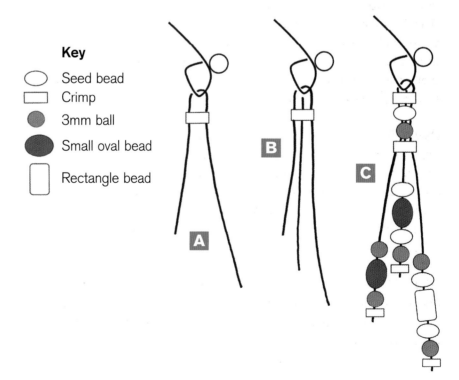

making **vintage** jewellery

josephine

EGYPTIAN NECKLACE WITH STONE DROPS

With the discovery of Tutankhamun's tomb in the early 1920s, all things Egyptian came into vogue – everything from scarab beetle motifs to Pharaoh-inspired collars.

This refined necklace sits flat like a collar and has echoes of the styles of ancient Egypt. There are two options – the collar can be made either with simple semi-precious stone blocks and drops for a more sophisticated look or with a wire pendant formed on a jig for added glamour (page 71).

you will need

* ✱ 19 size 6mm semi-precious stone beads for 'blocks'
* ✱ 3 'drop' shaped stone beads (approx 7 x 16 mm drilled top to bottom) for dangles
* ✱ Approx 150 bugle beads (approx 5g) size 7mm length
* ✱ 66in (165cm) of flexible beading wire/tiger tail
* ✱ 8 x 3-hole spacer bars
* ✱ 2 calottes
* ✱ 18 small crimps
* ✱ 1 fastener of your choice (barrel clasps have been used here)
* ✱ 2 jump rings
* ✱ 3 head pins

making up instructions

Step 1
Cut the tiger tail into three equal lengths of 22in (56cm) then, starting with the top strand, thread a crimp onto one length of tiger tail and squash approximately 2in (5cm) from one end.

Step 2
Thread on 16 bugle beads, go through the top hole of a spacer bar, thread on two 6mm stone beads, and go through the top hole of a second spacer bar.

Step 3
Thread on six bugle beads, go through the top hole of a third spacer bar, thread on two 6mm stone beads and go through the top hole of a fourth spacer bar.

Step 4
Continue the second side of the top string in the same way as the first by threading on six bugle beads, going through the top hole of the fifth spacer bar, threading on two 6mm stone beads and then going through the top hole of the sixth and final spacer bar.

Step 5
Thread on 16 bugle beads and finish by squashing a crimp after the last bugle. Leave the tail. **NB: Do not push the beads up too tightly before crimping.** Curve the strand and allow adequate hanging space.

Step 6
Proceed with the second row in the same manner as the first by crimping approximately 2in (5cm) from the end, threading on the appropriate number of bugle beads as shown in main diagram and this time going through the middle hole in the six spacer bars and threading on the two 6mm stone beads in between as you go. Crimp at the end as before and leave the tail.

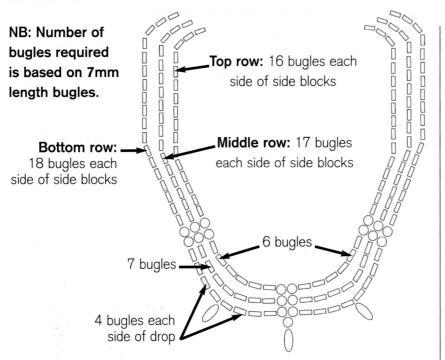

NB: Number of bugles required is based on 7mm length bugles.

Top row: 16 bugles each side of side blocks

Middle row: 17 bugles each side of side blocks

Bottom row: 18 bugles each side of side blocks

6 bugles

7 bugles

4 bugles each side of drop

Step 7

Make the three 'dangles' before you thread the bottom row. Thread a single stone 'drop' bead onto each of two head pins and make loops at the top (refer to **Making a Loop in Wire**, page 17). On the third head pin, thread first a 'drop' pearl, then a 6mm stone bead and turn a loop at the top.

Step 8

Make the bottom row in the same manner as the previous two, first by crimping approximately 2in (5cm) from the end, threading on the appropriate number of bugle beads as shown in the diagram and this time going through the bottom hole in the six spacer bars. This time though, thread on the single drop dangles in the appropriate places as shown above, and thread the long dangle between the two pearls in the

centre block. Crimp at the end as before and leave the tail.

Step 9

To finish, thread the tails through the holes of the two remaining spacer bars at each end of the collar. Secure the bottom and top strands with crimps (two on each for extra security) and cut off the tails. Note that there will be crimps both sides of the spacer bar. The centre strand will support the catch – therefore on the centre strand, thread a calotte on, then one or two crimps and squash firmly in place. Add a drop of glue, trim back tails and close the calotte over the crimps.

Step 10

Attach jump rings and catch to the calottes (refer to **Using End Findings**, page 16).

To make this version with a wire pendant on the front, you will have to make the pendant first following the diagrams and thread it between the two beads in the central block of the bottom strand of the collar. Suspend the pendant from a jump ring. You will need the same supplies to make this necklace, except you should omit the three drop-shaped stone beads and add the following instead.

you will need

* 12in (30cm) of 18 gauge wire (silver-plated/gold-plated or hobby wire)
* 3 short head pins
* 3 extra 6mm beads
* 6 seed beads
* 1 jump ring

Refer also to General Techniques for Using a Wire Jig, page 20.

Step 1

Begin by making a loop at one end of the wire using round nose pliers. **NB: The loop must be large enough to fit over the pegs in the wire jig.** Place the pegs in the wire jig in the pattern shown (**A**)

Step 2

Place the loop of the wire over the top peg in the pattern, with the loop facing to the left. Then wind the wire under the peg to the lower left and around it in a clockwise direction. Take the wire across the jig and under the peg to the right. Wrap it around the peg in an anti-clockwise direction (**B**).

Step 3

Move onto the next peg on the lower left, wrap clockwise then take the wire across the jig and under the peg on the right, wrapping around in an anti-clockwise direction (**C**). Remember as you wind to push the wire down your finger or a piece of dowelling.

Step 4

Continue to wrap under and round the lower two pegs in the same way, then finish by wrapping the wire in an anti-clockwise direction around the bottom peg to form a loop (**D**).

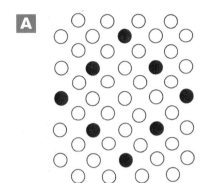

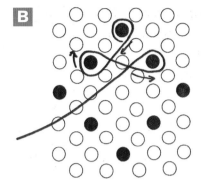

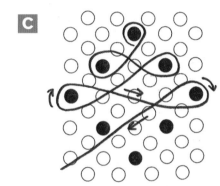

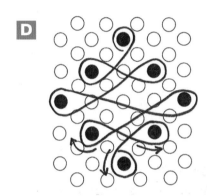

Step 5

Gently remove the pendant from the jig and trim the wire tail at the loop; flush with the wire next to it using wire cutters. You must now 'reshape' the pendant using a soft cloth and pliers to flatten it into the desired shape.

Step 6

Make three dangles for the pendant by threading a seed bead, 6mm stone bead and another seed bead onto each of the three head pins and turning a loop at the top. Attach the dangles to the two central/side loops of the pendant and the bottom loop (**E**). Remember to form the loop completely first then open/close it as you would a jump ring. Attach a jump ring to the top loop.

Step 7

Proceed by making the necklace as described in the stages above and thread the pendant on via the jump ring between the two 6mm stone beads in the front block of beads as you are threading the lower strand.

viola

EGYPTIAN DISC NECKLACE

This project makes a very unusual necklace which lays flat against the neck like a collar and has an Egyptian feel to it in keeping with the trends of the early 1920s. It offers the ideal use for the multitude of flat resin and wooden disc beads currently on the market.

Experiment with different colour combinations – this necklace looks understated made in the earthy browns on page 75 for example, compared to the distinctive lilac and olive combination shown here. I always receive comments when I wear my version of this necklace – it is striking without being ostentatious and is versatile enough to be worn as an accompaniment to almost any outfit.

making up instructions

Step 1

Start by making the seven supporting posts using your head pins. If using head pins cut the heads off all of the pins and turn a small secure loop at one end of each pin, using round nose pliers. If using eye pins then go straight onto **Step 2**.

Step 2

Thread on one 6mm faceted bead, one oval bead and another 6mm faceted bead onto four of the pins. Then turn another loop tight up against the last 6mm faceted bead so that you have a secure loop at each end of the pin. Make sure that all loops are facing the same direction and that there are no gaps in the loops (refer to **Making a Loop in Wire**, page 17).

Step 3

On the remaining three pins thread a disc bead and turn another loop at the other end tight up against the bead. Make sure that all the loops are facing the same direction and that there are no gaps in the loops. These are now your support blocks (**A**, page 74).

Step 4

Cut the tiger tail wire into two lengths of 24in (60cm). Start by threading the top row only. Thread one of the disc supports onto the middle of one wire. Thread a large (size 6) seed bead either side, then thread five small (size 11) seed beads either side. Thread another large seed bead either side, then thread an oval support each side. Repeat the pattern until you have threaded all supports alternately

you will need

* 3 wood or resin disc beads (size 20mm)

* 6 glass oval (lustre) beads (size 12 x 8mm approx)

* 110 approx large (size 6) seed beads

* 14 x 6mm faceted or hexagon beads

* 5 grams (approx) small (size 11) seed beads (approx 180 beads)

* 7 long eye pins or head pins

* 4–6 crimps

* 2 calottes

* 2 jump rings

* Fastener of your choice

* 48in (120cm) of tiger tail wire

You may have to adjust the quantity of large seeds beads used according to the size you use (6 or 8,).

(with five small seeds between and a large seed either side of each block pin). Then thread seven small seeds each side, another large seed each side, another seven small seeds each side, then finish with a large seed each side (refer to diagram **B** throughout these stages).

Step 5

Now thread the second strand. Take the second wire through the large seed at one end of the first strand (it may help to temporarily secure the strands together using tape). Then thread 10 small seeds, one large seed and 10 small seeds. Thread on one large seed then take the wire through the bottom loop on the first support block. Thread on another large seed the other side of the support block, then continue in this pattern of 10 small seeds between each block, and a large seed each side of each block (which will stabilize the necklace) until you have been through all support blocks and have reached the final large seed at the other side.

Key

○ Size 6 seed

⬭ Oval bead

⬤ 6mm facet

▭ Crimp

◯ Large disc

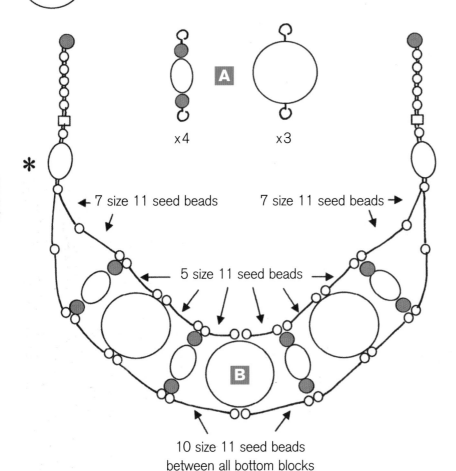

x4   x3

A

← 7 size 11 seed beads   7 size 11 seed beads →

← 5 size 11 seed beads →

B

10 size 11 seed beads
between <u>all</u> bottom blocks

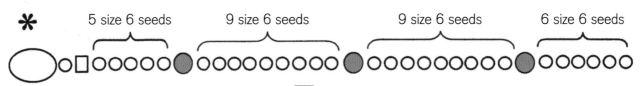

5 size 6 seeds   9 size 6 seeds   9 size 6 seeds   6 size 6 seeds

C

Step 6

Take the second wire through the large seed bead at this end of the first wire. Working with both wires together as one, thread both wires through an oval bead, a large seed and a crimp on each side.

Step 7

Adjust the tension of the necklace so that the front section will hang flat. Take your time and do not pull the beads up too tight. When happy with the arrangement, squash the crimp on each side to secure the necklace front section.

Step 8

Then threading onto both wires together as one, after the crimp on each side thread five large seeds and one 6mm faceted bead. Then on each side thread nine large seeds and a 6mm faceted, nine more large seeds and a 6mm faceted and finish with six more large seeds. (For slightly smaller seed beads like those used in the brown version of the necklace (see **Variations**, below), you should use 10 seeds, 6mm, 10 seeds, 6mm, and finish with 10 seeds (**C**).

Step 9

On each end, thread both wires through a calotte and one or two crimps. Squash the crimp, add a little glue and close the calotte over the top. Finally, close loops, add jump rings to each end and a fastener (refer to **Using End Findings**, page 16).

variations

The **brown** version of the necklace (pictured right) uses slightly **smaller seed beads** than the lilac version.

If you want a slightly **longer** necklace, you can adjust the quantity of **large seeds** used at each end of the necklace. Do not adjust the quantity of beads in the front section as these have been worked out to ensure that the necklace lays flat.

dimensions

Approximately 9in (23cm)
deep by 5½in (14cm) wide
(excluding handle)

templates

pages 151–152

suggested fabrics

for main bag fabric:
cotton velvet or silk brocade

for bag lining:
firm weight silk

madeline

ART DECO LONG EVENING PURSE

This purse can be classed as jewellery partly because of its long bead strap and chain tassel and since it can be worn across the body as a form of adornment. Long shaped purses with tasselled corners were popular in this decade along with amulet bags.

This ornamental but practical purse, with its asymmetric flap, can be made using small amounts of velvet or silk. It can be worn as part of an evening outfit in matching fabric and offers the ideal place to keep your essentials safe. It could also be made in less dressy fabrics, like wool with a wooden bead strap and tassel for day wear.

you will need

* 12in (30cm) of main fabric, 32in (82cm) wide
* 12in (30cm) of iron-on medium/heavy interfacing, 32in (82cm) wide
* 12in (30cm) of lining fabric, 16in (41cm) wide
* 94in (240cm) of tiger tail wire for the handle
* 133 x 6mm plastic round beads for handle
* 64 x 6mm glass round beads (50 for handle/14 for tassel)
* 3 large oval beads (for strap and tassel with large centre holes) size approx 10 x 20mm
* Approx 18in (46cm) of antiqued chain (large link)
* 1 long eye pin
* 6 small head pins
* 1 large jump ring
* 4 large crimps for handle
* 1 large cover button – 1¼in (30mm)
* Piece of fusible web 2 x 2in (5 x 5cm) for strap loops

cutting out

* Cut 2 x front/back from main fabric
* Cut 2 x front/back from interfacing
* Cut 2 x front/back from lining fabric
* Cut 2 x flap from main fabric (cut with wrong sides together)
* Cut 1 x flap from interfacing
* Cut 2 x strap loop from main fabric
* Cut 2 x strap loop from fusible web

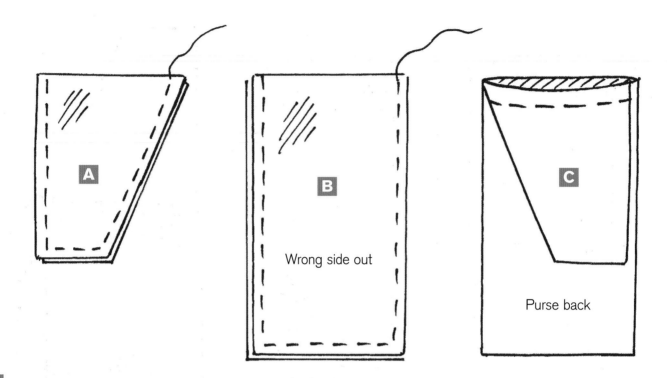

Wrong side out

Purse back

Step 1

Iron interfacing onto wrong sides of front and back pieces and one of the flap pieces.

Step 2

Now pin flap sections right sides together. Stitch together round side/lower edges marked with dotted line on pattern template, leaving a ½in (13mm) seam allowance (**A**). Trim seams, clip seam allowance at corners and turn right sides out. Press gently through a cloth. If you wish you can then top-stitch all around using a long stitch length.

Step 3

Pin the two interfaced front/back pieces right sides of main fabric together. Stitch around sides and lower edges, leaving a ½in (13mm) seam allowance (**B**). Trim the seam back to ³⁄₈in (1cm) to cut down on bulk. Turn bag right sides out and press.

Step 4

Pin the finished flap onto the back of the bag, right outside of flap against right outside of bag back, with raw edges even. Baste stitch approximately ½in (13mm) from the edge (**C**).

Step 5

Make strap loops. Iron fusible web onto reverse of both the strap loop pieces. Fold long outside edges

(marked with a dotted line on the pattern template) into the centre and fuse in place. Fold loops in half and with raw edges even stitch together about ½in (13mm) from the raw edge.

Step 6

On outside, positioned next to flap and centred over side seams with raw edges even, pin strap loops to bag facing downwards and with raw edges even. Baste in place (**D**).

Step 7

Stitch the lining pieces together at sides and lower edges, leaving an opening of around 4in (10cm) at centre of lower edge for turning.

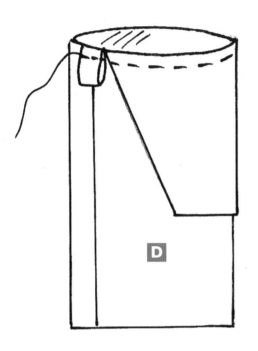

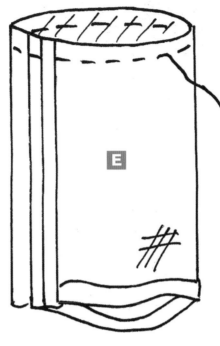

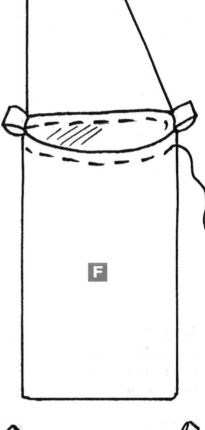

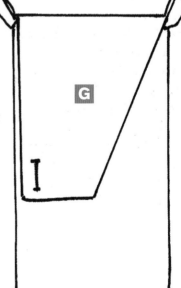

Step 8

With right sides together, insert bag into lining. Pin lining to bag and baste together around upper edges (with flap and strap loops sandwiched between). Stitch together leaving a little over ½in (13mm) seam allowance (**E**). Stitch slowly and carefully, especially over the handle loops. Trim the seam back to ⅜in (1cm) to eliminate bulk. Clip into seam allowance at sides.

Step 9

Turn the bag right side out through the opening in the bottom of the lining and slip-stitch the opening closed.

Step 10

Pull flap upwards and roll the lining with your fingers so that it is not visible from the outside, then pin and hand-baste it in place around upper edge of bag. Top-stitch through all layers, a little over ½in (13mm) from the top of the bag, using a long stitch length and taking extra care when sewing through the bulkier areas (**F**). Close the flap and then give a final light press.

Step 11

Make a button-hole at the position marked on the pattern piece to fit your cover button (**G**). Cover the button with velvet and stitch to bag at correct position.

to make the handle and tassel

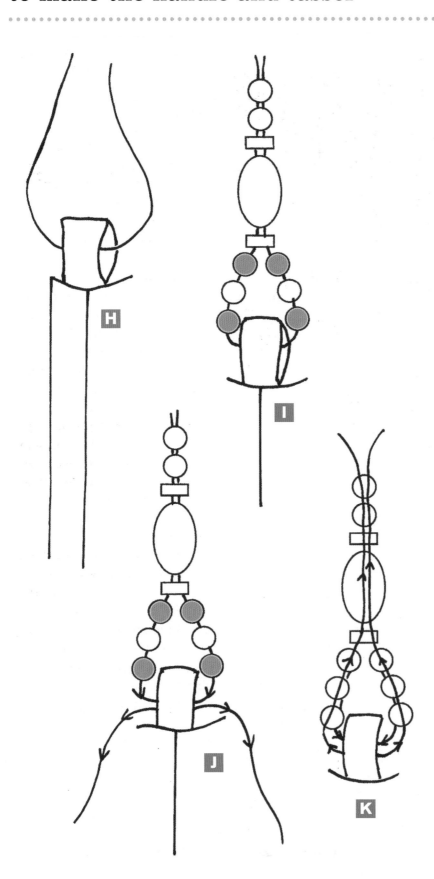

Step 12
Thread the length of tiger tail wire through the strap loop on the left of the purse so that both ends of the wire are even (**H**). On either tail thread one 6mm glass bead, one 6mm plastic bead and another 6mm glass bead. Next take both tails together through a crimp bead, a large oval bead and another crimp bead. Push the beads up close so that they form a triangular shape, then squash the crimps in place (**I**).

Step 13
Now working with both wires as one, thread on a pattern of three 6mm plastic beads and one 6mm glass bead until you have threaded 42 glass beads and 43 blocks of three plastic beads.

Step 14
After the last block of plastic beads, thread both wires through a crimp, a large oval bead and another crimp. Separate the wires and on each wire thread a 6mm glass bead, a 6mm plastic bead and another 6mm glass bead. Take the wires in opposite directions through the strap loop (**J**) on the right-hand side of the bag and up through the opposite beads, up through the crimp, oval bead, second crimp and a few more beads (**K**). Pull both wires up fairly tightly but ensure that you allow adequate hanging space so that the strap is not 'stiff'. When you have an arrangement that you are happy with, squash the crimps firmly to secure the handle in place

▲ You could use this tassel to make a fabulous sautoir necklace or make smaller versions as earrings.

and trim the wire ends taking care not to cut any supporting wires.

Step 15

Make the tassel. On the large eye pin, thread a 6mm glass bead, a large oval bead and another 6mm glass bead. Turn a loop above the glass bead referring to **Making a Loop in Wire**, page 17. There will now be a loop at each end.

Step 16

Thread one 6mm glass bead onto each of the 12 short head pins and turn a loop above each. Cut the chain into six uneven lengths using wire cutters. Attach a 6mm bead dangle to the bottom link and to the second from bottom link of each chain length. Open the loop at the bottom of the oval bead eye-pin link. Attach all of the six chain sections to this loop via the top link on each chain length.

Step 17

Open the jump ring and attach it to the top loop on the tassel and while the ring is open attach it at the base of the triangular bead formation just above the strap loop on the right side of the purse, hanging towards the front.

variations

This lightweight purse is suited to a beaded strap, but if you do not wish to make a feature of the beaded strap you could use decorative **rope** or **cording** (designed for use in furnishing trims) instead.

You could also use an **ornamental clasp** or **vintage button**, a **beaded fringe** along the lower edge of the purse or perhaps **tassels** at each of the lower corners.

The chain tassel on the handle of this bag could also be used on a long **necklace**.

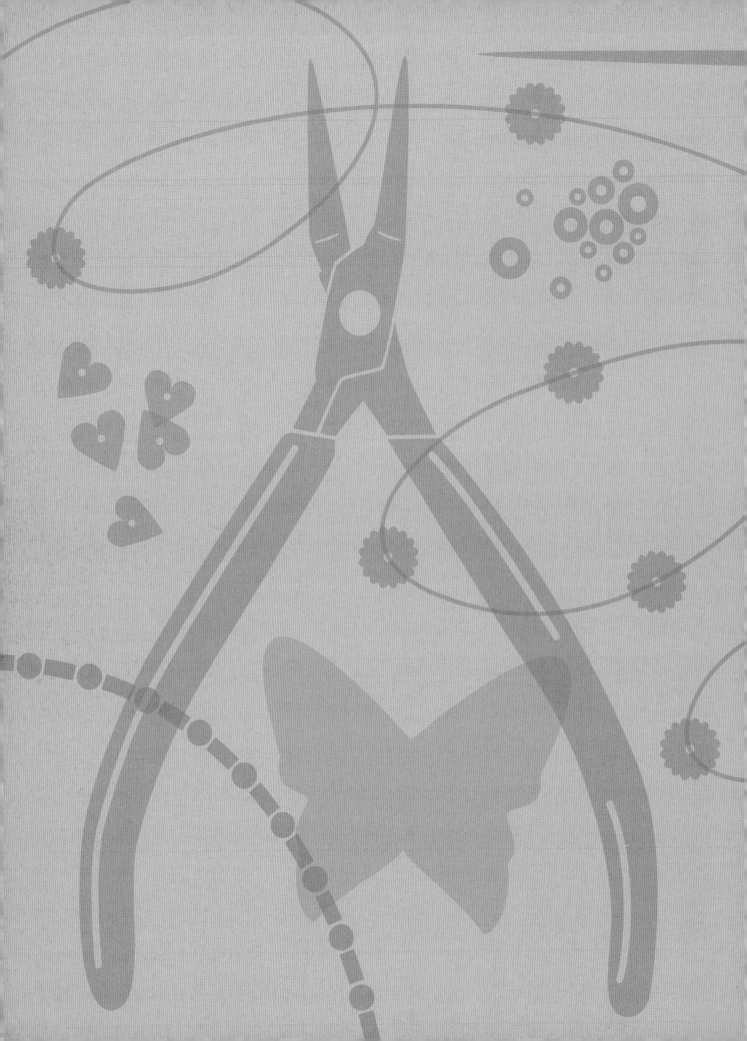

1930s

meredith

1930s NET WEAVE CHOKER

In the 1930s bold construction and geometrical patterns were very evident in jewellery design. This choker is made following a 'net weave' pattern of construction, which can be adapted for use with different materials. It has all the glamour and simplicity of the 30s era but still retains a contemporary feel.

This choker is made using good quality flexible beading wire but it could also be made with 28 gauge wire instead of tiger tail, which will allow you to shape it when it is finished. Alternatively, you could also use aged bronze or copper finish 3mm balls and findings instead of the silver to give the necklace a more antique look.

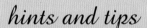

hints and tips

The materials listed opposite will make a choker that is approximately 14½in (37cm) in length.

Note that the diagram on page 86 stops at the middle of the choker – when you reach the middle of your choker, turn the pattern around and make the other half. (It is a continuation and mirror image of the first half, from the centre point.)

you will need

* 96 x 7mm smoky grey bugle beads

* 96in (240cm) of tiger tail wire cut into 4 lengths of 24in (60cm)

* 6 silver-coloured tubes with large holes

* 6 x 6mm smoky grey faceted glass beads with large holes

* 40 x 3mm silver-coloured balls (or beads)

* 2 large crimps (or 4 small)

* 2 large calottes

* 2 jump rings

* Fastener of your choice

making up instructions

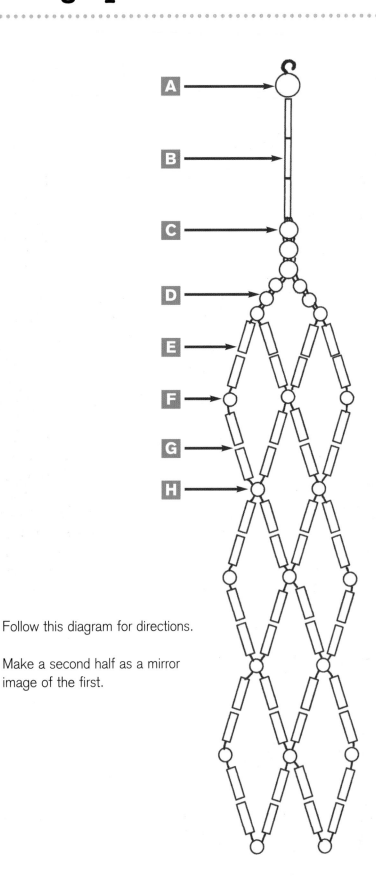

Follow this diagram for directions.

Make a second half as a mirror image of the first.

Step 1
Start the choker by attaching all four wires together at one end. Crimp the wires together either in pairs using one small crimp per pair of wires, or crimp all four wires together using one large crimp.

Step 2
Hold the two pairs of wire together, crimps on top of each other, add a blob of glue and then close a large calotte over the two crimps, thus securing all four wires together (**A**). **NB: You can use a large side-fastening calotte for this choker or a traditional clam shell**. Refer to **Using End Findings**, page 16, for more help.

Step 3
Next thread all four wires together through three large-holed metal tubes (**B**).

Step 4
Thread all four wires together through three large-holed faceted glass 6mm beads (**C**). Split the wires into two pairs and thread each pair of wires through three 3mm silver balls (**D**).

Step 5
Now split the wires out singly so that you have four working wires and add two 7mm bugle beads onto each of the four wires (**E**).

Step 6

Add a 3mm silver ball onto each outside wire and thread both centre wires together through a single silver ball in the middle (**F**).

Step 7

Add two bugles onto each of the four wires (**G**). Add a silver ball onto each outside wire and bring each centre wire out and thread through the silver balls on the outside wires (**H**). Continue by adding two bugles onto each of the four wires.

Step 8

Add a 3mm silver ball onto each outside wire and thread both centre wires together through a single silver ball in the middle.

Step 9

Follow the diagram repeating this pattern until you have completed 11 lines of silver balls (six rows of three and five rows of two). **NB: Only half of the choker is shown on the diagram.**

Step 10

Finish the choker by repeating the start in reverse. Add fastenings onto the choker using the jump rings. You may wish to add an 'extender chain' or extra jump rings to allow for neck size variation.

variations

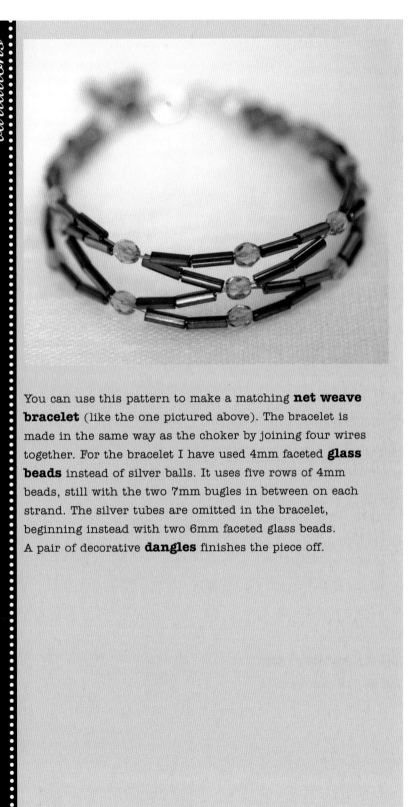

You can use this pattern to make a matching **net weave bracelet** (like the one pictured above). The bracelet is made in the same way as the choker by joining four wires together. For the bracelet I have used 4mm faceted **glass beads** instead of silver balls. It uses five rows of 4mm beads, still with the two 7mm bugles in between on each strand. The silver tubes are omitted in the bracelet, beginning instead with two 6mm faceted glass beads. A pair of decorative **dangles** finishes the piece off.

meredith

1930s

elsie

BRAIDED MEDLEY NECKLACE

Necklaces in the 1930s tended to be shorter than their predecessors and quite dressy. This was because of the new emphasis on more shapely figures, to which the long sautoir necklaces of the previous decade were not so well suited.

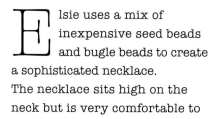

lsie uses a mix of inexpensive seed beads and bugle beads to create a sophisticated necklace. The necklace sits high on the neck but is very comfortable to wear – making it from 34 gauge wire makes it even more flexible. Try out different beads including glass flowers or semi-precious stone chips for an alternative look.

you will need

* 168in (approx 426cm) of 28 or 34 gauge wire cut into 3 lengths of 56in (142cm)

* 65 bugle beads in one colour (size 6mm)

* 65 bugle beads in a second colour (size 6mm)

* Approx 260 seed beads (size 10) in one colour

* Approx 210 size 8 seed beads in second colour

* 11 or 12 lozenge-shaped beads

* 20 size 6mm beads

* 2 bell end caps

* 2 eye pins

* 2–4 jump rings

* Clasp of your choice

hints and tips

These instructions are based on making a six-strand necklace. If you plait the stands together loosely, the quantities of beads given will make a necklace that has a finished length of approximately 16in (41cm). If you plait and twist the strands more tightly, the necklace will have a finished length of approximately 15in (38cm).

Be careful not to get kinks or sharp bends in the wire while you work. This will make it more likely to break. If the wire breaks in this design, you will not be able to rectify it by working in a new piece. Work on one strand at a time and take your time making the loops around the beads to secure them.

making up instructions

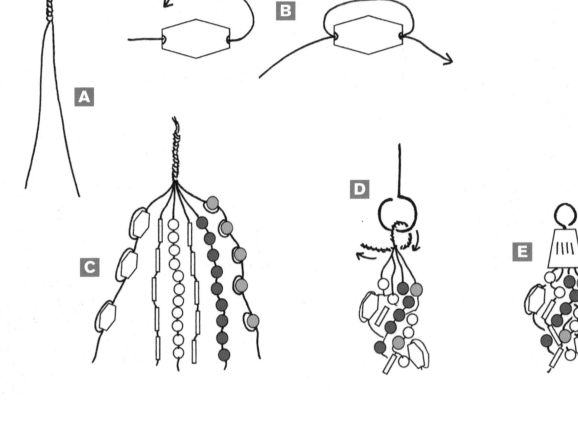

Step 1

Start by taking each wire individually and folding it in half. Then twist the folded end around itself to create a 2in (5cm) tail (**A**). This will mean that you have six strands to work with (or three pairs).

Step 2

Work one strand at a time. On the first strand, thread on 65 bugles, and then bend the end of the wire back to prevent the bugles falling off while you work. On the second strand, thread on size 10 seed beads until you have beaded the

same length as the bugles. After the last seed bead, tie a loose knot in the wire up against it to prevent the seed beads falling off while you continue to work.

Step 3

On the second pair of strands, thread 65 of your second colour bugles onto the first strand, and on the second, thread on size 8 seed beads until you have beaded the same length as the bugles. After the last seed bead, tie a loose knot in the wire up against it to prevent the seed beads falling off while you continue to work.

Step 4

Next work on the third pair of wires. On the first strand thread a lozenge bead about 1in (25mm) from the end. Take the wire around the bead and back through the hole again in the same direction so that it is secured in place (**B**). Leave a space of about 1in (25mm), then thread another. Repeat until you have threaded and secured all 11 or 12 beads in place. On the last strand, follow the same procedure, but thread and secure all 20 of the 6mm beads in place. Thread them a little closer together than the lozenges.

Because this necklace has six strands it offers a great way to experiment with unusual blends of colours. It looks very different made in the **smoky grey and mauve** version (pictured), for example.

For an alternative look you could use a decorative **end cap** and a **fancy clasp** (a toggle clasp for example) and have it at the front of the necklace, with some **decorative dangles**. This method of construction could also be used to make a **bracelet**. You could even work in extra strands of wire to make the bracelet **chunkier**.

Step 5

When all six strands are beaded, twist the tails of the three pairs of beaded strands together to form a single twisted tail. All six strands should now be joined together at one end (**C**).

Step 6

Next take three strands – one bugle, one seed and one larger bead strand – and plait (braid) them together loosely. If you braid too tightly the necklace will be too stiff and will not have enough movement in it. Next, twist the three wire ends together to secure the braiding. Repeat this process with the other three strands.

Step 7

Finally, take the two plaits and twist them together. Secure all wire tails by twisting together as you did with the other end. Cut both twisted tails down to around 1in (25mm).

Step 8

Thread the twisted wire tail through an eye pin at each end and wrap the wire tail around the pin securely, trimming if necessary (**D**). Thread a bell end cap onto the pin so that the bell covers the wire completely. Turn a loop in the eye pin, close up against the bell cap (**E**). Refer also to **Finishing Off with Fine Wire**, page 23.

Step 9

Fix clasp to turned loop using the jump rings.

rosaline

RIBBON ROSE WIRE CHOKER

This beautiful choker is one of my favourite projects because it combines the vintage style decorative textile element of the ribbon roses perfectly with the harder edge of contemporary wire work. The result is a unique structured neckpiece with a softer, romantic side.

The glass leaf hanging from the back of the choker is also in keeping with the 1930s trend for ornamental elements suspended from a clasp. The purchased roses for this piece have been hand-painted with fabric dye so that they blend delicately with the tones of the beads. The olive-green coated wire shows up more than a silver or gold wire would, making a bold 30s-style statement.

you will need

* ✱ 5 x ¾in (19mm) ribbon roses (with leaves)
* ✱ 140in (360cm) of 26 gauge wire cut into 2 lengths of 70in (180cm)
* ✱ Large lobster clasp
* ✱ 1 solid jump ring
* ✱ 7 large crimps
* ✱ 6 medium sized jump rings
* ✱ Approx 48 x 6mm beads with large holes
* ✱ Approx 100 large (size 6) seed beads
* ✱ 1 large glass leaf bead
* ✱ Sewing thread to match roses and a needle

making up instructions

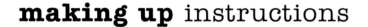

Step 1

Start by taking both of the 70in (180cm) wires together through the hole in the lobster clasp. Find the centre of the wires and fold them in half over the clasp so that you have four equal length pieces of wire to work with. Then thread all four wires through one large crimp. Push the crimp up fairly tight against the clasp and squash it securely, taking care not to break any of the wires (**A**).

Step 2

Work all four strands at the same time. Begin by threading two seed beads onto the first wire. Next thread on a 6mm bead about 1¼in (3cm) from the end, take the wire around the bead and back through the hole again in the same direction, thus securing it in place (**B**). Add two further seed beads, then another 6mm bead approximately 1¼in (3cm) from the first and secure in the same way as the first. Do the same for all four strands of wire. **NB: The seed beads will remain 'loose' in between the 6mm beads**.

Step 3

Next thread all four wires through a large crimp. This crimp should be 2½–3in (6–7.5cm) from the end crimp. Squash the crimp firmly to secure the wires in place – be careful not to break any of the wires with the pliers. Fan out the four wires to form a 'scallop' effect (**C**).

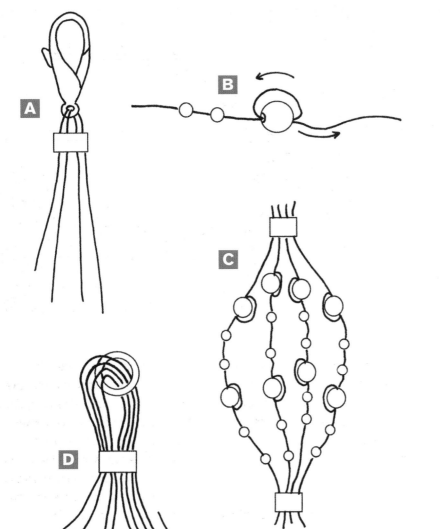

Stitch here

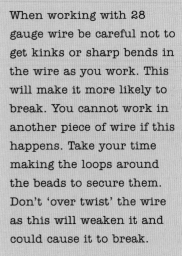

When working with 28 gauge wire be careful not to get kinks or sharp bends in the wire as you work. This will make it more likely to break. You cannot work in another piece of wire if this happens. Take your time making the loops around the beads to secure them. Don't 'over twist' the wire as this will weaken it and could cause it to break.

Step 4

For the next section, thread the same number of seed beads and 6mm beads onto each of the four strands, securing as before and using the same spacing. Take all wires through another crimp, which should be around 2½–3in (6–7.5cm) from the previous crimp. Squash the crimp firmly to secure the wires in place as before, taking extreme care not to break any of the wires.

Step 5

Continue making scallops in this way until you have made six of them and then thread all four wires through a crimp. Push the crimp up so that it is 2½–3in (6–7.5cm) from the previous crimp as before. Take all wires through a closed jump ring and then thread them back through the crimp (**D**). (Refer also to the section on

The alternative **'loopy'** version of this choker is more funky and modern and can be made using any combination of beads and loops. As a more **contemporary** and random piece than the rose choker, it is perfect for using up different sized beads in the same shade. The 'loops' are small **lingerie rings** that are secured in place by wrapping the wire around them in between **scallops** instead of using crimps. The large glass beads and the sequins are secured in place in the same way as the 6mm beads in the rose choker.

variations

Finishing Off with Fine Wire, on page 23, for further help.)

Step 6

Push the wire tails through together, but gently pull them one by one to ease the strands up tight to form a loop over the jump ring.

Step 7

When you are happy with the loop, squash the crimp in place taking care not to break any of the strands, and then wrap the tails of the wire around the crimp and supporting wires several times. Cut off the tails of two strands and wrap the remaining two strands around several times to cover the two ends. Clip the final tails and hide in the wrap.

Step 8

Join the six jump rings together in a chain then add them to the closed jump ring. This 'chain' will be used to fasten the necklace and will make it more multi-sized. Attach the glass leaf bead to the bottom jump ring in the chain for decoration.

Step 9

You must now stitch the five ribbon roses to the choker over the top of the five crimps in the scallops. Thread a needle with a double thickness of thread and, making a knot at one end, attach the needle/thread to a rose. With the rose on the right side stitch it to the choker from the reverse side, over and around all of the wires both sides of the crimp (**E**). This will keep the roses lying flat and secure and will cover the crimps.

Step 10

Finish off the choker by twisting the wire in between the beads. Do this by grasping the wire with round nose pliers and twisting the pliers in a clockwise direction, thus twisting the wire in an 'S' shape. Hold the pliers with the points downwards and support the wires in the palm of your hand. Twist the wire once or twice on each strand in each scallop in a random manner between beads. **NB: Twisting the wire in this way will lose around 2in (5cm) from the overall length of the choker** (refer to **Working with Fine Gauge Wire**, page 22, for help with this technique).

Step 11

When you have finished, do the choker up and shape it either on a neck bust or try it on and gently bend the wire to shape it accordingly.

wanda

RANDOM WEAVE BRACELET

Fashions for bracelets in the 1930s included carved or moulded plastic bangles and geometric designs in metals set with fake stones. However, many of the carved pieces also followed flowing, draped and twisted designs.

This contemporary bracelet is made by threading wire through different sized beads of a similar shade in a random 'net' type weave. The wire is 'twisted' after the bracelet has been assembled (as in **Rosaline**, page 93) to add to the 'unsystematic' look. The project offers a good way to use readily available packets of random size Indian glass beads. It could also be made using vintage glass beads, or a large focal art bead if you wanted to creat a more retro look.

you will need

* 120in (3m) of 28 gauge silver-coloured wire, cut into 3 lengths of 40in (1m)
* Approx 60 transparent large seed beads (size 6) with large centre holes
* Approx 20 glass beads of random size and shape, in toning colours (in this case, pink, with a large central feature bead)
* 2 eye pins
* 2 bell end caps
* 2–4 jump rings
* Bolt ring or small lobster fastener

making up instructions

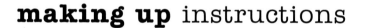

Step 1

Start by taking each 40in (1m) wire and folding it in half. Then twist the folded end around itself to create a 2in (5cm) tail. This will mean that you have six strands to work with (or three pairs). See **Elsie**, page 88, for illustrations of this.

Step 2

Work one strand at a time. On the first strand thread a seed bead and about 1in (25mm) from the twisted end, take the wire around the bead and back through the hole again in the same direction so that it is secured in place. Thread on another seed or glass bead and secure in place as before. The space between the beads should be around ½in (13mm). Repeat the first step until you have threaded

hints and tips

The materials listed (right) are based on making a six-strand woven bracelet. As the wire passes through most beads at least twice, you must make sure that you use beads with holes that are large enough to take three to four wires.

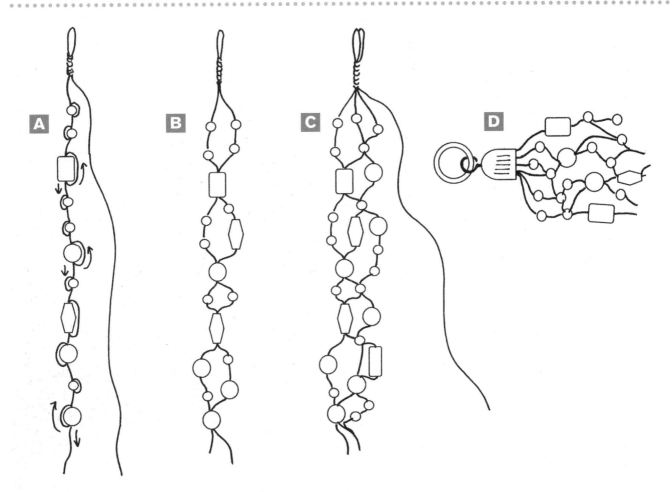

and secured a mixture of 11 or 12 seed and glass beads in place. The distance between the first and last beads threaded should be around 5in (13cm), with a 1in (2.5cm) tail at the beginning (you will leave 1in (2.5cm) at the end afterwards). **NB: Secure all beads threaded on the first strand (A).**

Step 3

On the second strand, follow the same procedure, but secure the first bead only ½in (13mm) from the end and then take the wire through (or pick up) one of the beads from the first strand, and go round it and through it again to secure. Add another one or two

beads, securing some of them, then take the wire through another bead on the first strand. Proceed in this manner until you have reached the end of the first wire, and then lightly twist the tails of the first two wires together. **NB: You should 'pick up' about five beads from the first strand (B).**

Step 4

Take the next pair of wires and lightly twist the looped tail around the looped tail of the first two beaded strands. Thread one or two beads onto the third strand and secure, then take the wire through one of the beads on the second strand. You will now be

starting to build up a random 'net' style weave (C). Complete the fourth strand in the same way, then twist on the third pair of wires and complete these in the same way.

Step 5

When you have woven all six strands together and used all the beads you want, twist the tails of all six strands together to form one tail, and cut back to about 1in (2.5cm). Do the same at the other end.

Step 6

Thread twisted wire tail through an eye pin at each end and wrap the wire tail around the pin securely, trimming off any excess. Thread a bell end cap onto the pin so that the bell covers the wire completely. Turn a loop in the eye pin, close up against the bell cap (**D**). (See **Elsie**, page 88, for further help with this step.) Refer also to **Finishing Off with Fine Wire**, page 23.

Step 7

Fix clasp to turned loop using the jump rings. The whole of the clasp (including rings and bell cap) will add around 1½in (38mm) to the overall length of the bracelet.

Step 8

At this point, the bracelet should be about 1½in (38mm) too long. You will now 'twist' the wire in between the beads. Do this by grasping the wire with round nose pliers and twisting the pliers in a clockwise direction, thus twisting the wire in an 'S' shape. Hold the pliers with the points downward and support the wires in the palm of your hand. Twist the wire once or twice on each strand in each scallop in a random manner between beads. **NB: Twisting the wire in this way will lose around 1½in (38mm) from the overall length of the bracelet.** (Refer to **Working with Fine Gauge Wire**, page 22).

variations

The **brown bracelet** (pictured above) was made following the same technique but instead of using large seed beads in between the focal glass beads, I have used all **larger beads** to give a more sparse but chunky look. There were around 38 beads used in this bracelet, none of them smaller than 6mm. The wire used has a **copper-coloured** finish to tone with the beads.

You could also make the random net weave base for the bracelet using only **seed beads** and then you could tie or stitch some **textile elements** to the wire in between as focal points. The wonderful thing about the unmethodical nature of this piece is that no two bracelets will ever come out exactly the same!

ruby

RIBBON AND WIRE FLOWER CORSAGE

This stunning 1930s inspired flower corsage would make the perfect showpiece for a ball or wedding outfit, pinned at the shoulder of a timeless evening dress or to secure a velvet shawl.

The flower petals are made from satin ribbon and the striking centrepiece is woven from wire and vintage glass beads. The black marabou feathers toning with the beads finish this statement piece perfectly. With the wonderful array of vintage and modern ribbons available today, including sumptuous jacquard weaves, fancy checks and jaunty grosgrain stripes, the possibilities with this flower design are infinite. Try making it with looped ribbon dangles instead of the dressy feathers for a more informal look.

you will need

✱ 30in (76cm) of satin ribbon, 1½in (38mm) wide for petals

✱ Cluster of fluffy marabou feathers for leaves

✱ Piece of felt 4 x 2½in (10 x 6.5cm) for base

✱ Piece of buckram 2in square (5cm square) for base

✱ Brooch backing bar with holes for sewing

✱ Needle and thread to match ribbon

For the flower centre

✱ Approx 150 seed beads (size 10 or 11) for petals

✱ 10 x 4mm faceted beads for petal tips

✱ Vintage faceted centre bead (approx 10mm)

✱ 16 size 8 seed beads for central circle

✱ 50in (127cm) of 28 gauge beading wire

making up instructions

the flower

The first part of making the base for this corsage is illustrated with photographs in **Corsages and Other Textile Projects**, page 30.

Step 1
First make a base for the corsage. Using the circular pattern templates from **Bessie**, page 45, cut out two corsage base pieces from felt and one corsage base buckram piece from buckram.

Step 2
Place the buckram circle centrally in between the two felt circles. Pin in the centre, then using a short machine stitch, sew circles together around the outside edge, about ¼in (6mm) from the outside edge.

Step 3
For each petal, cut a length of ribbon four times as long as the width. So for 1½in (38mm) wide ribbon, cut 6in (15cm) of ribbon. Fold the length of ribbon in half so that the cut ends are together.

Step 4
Tack the cut edges together with a gathering thread (**A**), pull up the gathers, secure the gathers with a few stitches at one side, then go back through the gathers again and secure at the other side. Make five petals in this way.

Step 5
On each petal fold in the top corners of the ribbon and tack together as in diagram **B**. (Don't go through to the front layer of ribbon.)

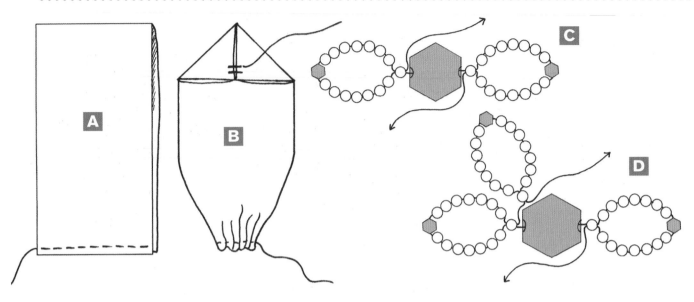

Step 6

You can now stitch the petals directly onto the corsage base. First bundle and tie the feathers together and stitch to the base with the quills in the centre so they will be covered by the petals. (See **Bessie**, page 45, for more help with this.)

Step 7

Fold under the gathered edge of each petal and arrange the petals around the outside of the base in a flower shape. The side edges of the petals will overlap slightly and the points of the petals will overhang the base by 1¾in (4.5cm) and there will be a small space in the middle of the petals about ⅜in (1cm) in diameter. Hand-stitch the petals in place, at the bottom (gathered) edge of each petal to the felt base and at the side edges of each petal to each other. Also stitch to the base around the edge of the base, trying not to come through to the front of the petal with the thread.

Step 8

Stitch a brooch bar on the back of the corsage base, at the centre top so that the corsage will not hang down when pinned onto clothing.

flower centre

Refer to **Working with Fine Gauge Wire**, page 22, for help with this part of the project.

Step 9

Take the 50in (127cm) length of beading wire and thread on the large 10mm centre bead to the centre of the wire. On one tail, thread on a small seed bead, thread on a further seven seed beads, one 4mm faceted bead, a further seven seed beads, then take the wire back down through the first seed bead in the opposite direction to form a loop/petal. Push the seed bead petal so that it is up against the 10mm bead in the centre of the wire.

Step 10

On the other wire tail repeat what you have just done with the first petal by threading on a small seed bead, a further seven seed beads, one 4mm faceted bead, a further seven seed beads, then take the wire back down through the first seed bead in the opposite direction. Push the seed bead petal up against the centre (10mm) bead so that you have one petal on either side (**C**).

Step 11

With one wire tail make another petal (**D**), then make three more so that you have five petals on one side. Then take the tail of this wire back through the large centre bead in a circle and pull up tight.

Step 12

Repeat the petal formation in steps **C** and **D** with the wire on the opposite side of the centre bead then take the wire tail through the centre bead in a circle (in the opposite direction to the first wire)

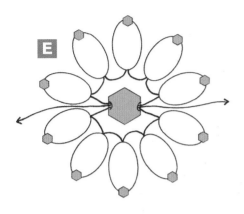

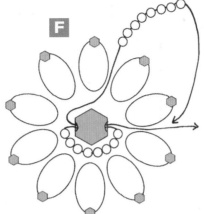

and pull up tight (**E**). **NB: In diagram E and onwards the seed beads are not shown on the petals.**

Step 13

On one wire, thread enough seed beads to encircle half of the central bead. If they are size 8 seed beads, it should take about 16 to encircle a 10mm bead (eight on each side). Next take the wire back through the centre bead in a circle (**F**). Repeat this with the other tail, then take the tail through the centre bead in the opposite direction to the first (**G**).

Step 14

To finish off the flower centre, wrap the wire tails a few times around the base of one of the petals on either side then trim the tails (making sure that you do not cut any of the supporting wires). As this will be stitched onto a ribbon flower with a felt base, the wire ends will be underneath and hidden, so they will not catch on anything. If you were making this

as a pendant, you should hide the ends of the wire inside one of the beads and cut back the tails, taking care not to cut any of the supporting wires.

Step 15

Finally, stitch the flower centre to the ribbon flower in the middle. Stitch round each supporting wire at the base of each petal.

ruby

103

1930s

1940s

marcia

ROSY DROP NECKLACE

Because of the limited availability of materials during the war years, jewellery in the 1940s tended to be quite innovative. This delightfully simple necklace is made on a base of cotton thong and sports a ribbon rose at the front with glass lozenge bead drops. A few smaller toning glass beads dotted around the neck add to the charm of this uncomplicated 40s-style piece.

Cotton thong makes the ideal foil for a pretty patterned ribbon, like the Burberry-type check used here – it only takes a few beads to accentuate the colours of the ribbon. You could also consider using a purchased ribbon flower instead of making your own. This necklace would make a great spring accessory in the neck of a crisp white cotton shirt.

you will need

* 84in (215cm) of cotton thong (1mm diameter) cut into 3 lengths of 20in (50cm) and 2 lengths of 12in (30cm)

* Approx 14in (36cm) of patterned ribbon, ⅝in (16mm) wide or a purchased ribbon rose with a diameter approx 1in (25mm)

* 4 lozenge-shaped glass beads with large holes

* 10 assorted 4mm or 6mm glass beads with large holes

* 12 large crimps

* 2 large lace-end crimps

* 2 large jump rings

* 1 bolt ring clasp

* For dangle – glass leaf, 4 small jump rings, 1 eye pin and 1 x 4mm bead

* Matching sewing thread and a needle

making up instructions

hints and tips

The materials listed (left) will make a necklace that is approximately 16½in (42cm) long.

All of the beads and crimps used in this project must have holes large enough for the cotton cord to pass through them easily.

Step 1

Cut the cotton thong into the appropriate lengths according to the materials list, left. Lay the three 20in (50cm) lengths together and find the centre point. Next take the two shorter lengths and fold them over the centre point of the three lengths in a larks head knot (**A**, **B** and **C**). You will now have four tails hanging down from the centre of the necklace.

Step 2

Next make a ribbon rose with the length of ribbon (if you are making your own). To do this, take the length of ribbon and roll one end over three or four times to form a centre then hand-stitch through all layers at the base of the rose. Next twist the ribbon spirally and secure

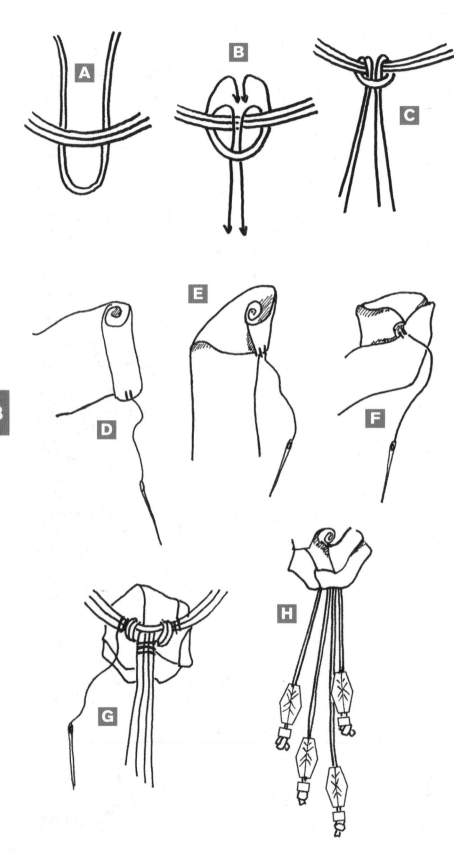

it with stitches at the base each time it is folded. Once you have a rose the size you need, cut the remaining ribbon, fold the raw edge under and stitch in place (**D**, **E** and **F**).

Step 3

Stitch the rose to the larks head knot in the centre of the necklace. Lay the rose on the front of the necklace and stitch from behind. Stitch around the four dangling cords all together and the main necklace cords at either side (**G**).

Step 4

Next on one of the main strands thread a large crimp and squash it approximately 1¼in (3cm) from the rose. Thread and squash a crimp in the same position on the same strand the other side of the rose. Now thread on two 4mm glass beads each side of the necklace.

Step 5

On the next strand on both sides thread and squash a crimp approximately 3in (8cm) from the rose, and then thread on a 4 or 6mm glass bead. On the third strand, on both sides, thread on and squash a crimp approximately 2¼in (6cm) from the ribbon rose. Thread on a 4 or 6mm bead. Finally, on both sides of the same strand thread another crimp and squash approximately 4¼in (11cm) from the rose. Thread on a final 4 or 6mm bead.

Step 6

Making sure that all three strands are even cut them down to approximately 7¾in (20cm) from the rose on each side. At each end, bind the three strands together with sewing thread, add a dab of glue then attach a lace-end crimp (refer to **Leather and Cotton Thong**, page 25).

Step 7

At one end attach the fastener to the lace end using one of the large jump rings. At the other end attach the other large jump ring to the lace end. If you wish to make a dangle, the one on this necklace has a glass leaf with a small jump ring attached to the top. A 4mm bead has been threaded onto an eye pin and another loop has been turned above it (refer to **Making a Loop in Wire**, page 17). The other three small jump rings have been joined together in a chain and the head-pin bead link has been attached to the glass leaf via the small jump ring.

Step 8

Finally, on each of the four front hanging strands of cotton cord, thread a glass lozenge bead and a large crimp bead. Squash the crimps to secure the beads in place, making sure that all of the beads hang at different levels so that all four tails are uneven. Directly under each crimp tie a small tight knot in the thong. Trim off the tails of the thong (**H**).

The alternative version of this necklace (pictured) was made using striking **black and white striped** grosgrain ribbon for the rose. Instead of having lozenge beads as drops, I have attached a small **lace-end crimp** to each of the four front tails and then attached a **glass leaf** bead to each lace end crimp, with a jump ring. At intervals around the neck I have used some **striped horn beads** with a large crimp at each end. The decorative **heart-shaped T-bar clasp** adds another point of difference.

You could also consider using fine **leather lace** instead of the cotton thong for a different look. You could make one of the **wired flowers** in this book (those featured in **Florence**, page 39 or **Ruby**, page 100 for example) to replace the ribbon rose and wire it to the larks head knot instead of stitching it.

constance

ASYMMETRIC PEARL LARIAT NECKLACE

Because the production of high-end jewellery came to a standstill during the war, 1940s minimalism gave rise to many simple, elegant and understated designs, often with asymmetric styling.

This shorter lariat-style necklace uses naturally shaped freshwater pearls against a backdrop of simple black cotton cord with silver coloured findings and spacer beads. This adaptable necklace would lift even the plainest shirt or V-necked sweater for elegant day wear – it would be equally at home with an elegant little black cocktail dress.

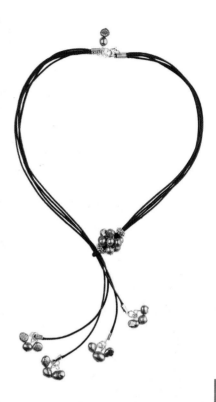

making up instructions

Step 1
Start by making the pearl cluster. Make the pearl bead 'cluster' by following steps **A** to **E**. Thread three pearls onto the centre of the length of 28 gauge beading wire. Then take both wire tails in opposite directions through the centre of a fourth pearl to form a circle (**A**).

Step 2
Pick up another pearl on each wire tail (**B**) then cross the tails in opposite directions through another pearl (**C**). Repeat this again, and then add another pearl onto each tail (**D**).

Step 3
Finally, take both wire tails and thread them in opposite directions through the very first centre pearl threaded at the other end (**E**). Pull the wires up tight and this will form a pearl ball or cluster. If the holes in

the beads are large enough, thread the wires back through adjacent beads in the opposite direction – wrap the wires around the supporting wires on each side, then clip the tails and hide them inside a bead if possible. If not, just wrap around the supporting wires and clip the tails carefully. (Refer to **Working with Fine Gauge Wire**, page 22.)

Step 4
Cut two pieces of cotton cord, each of 16in (41cm) in length. From the remainder, cut two lengths of approximately 12in (30.5cm) and two of approximately 10in (25cm).

Step 5
Hold the two 16in (41cm) lengths of cord and fold them in half so that all four cut ends are even. Attach the cut ends together by binding or stitching them with thread, then add

you will need

* Approx 84in (215cm) of 1mm cotton cord or leather thong

* 26 freshwater pearl beads (holes large enough to go through head pins)

* 2 large-hole silver-coloured spacer beads

* 13 small head pins

* 4 small lace-end crimps

* 7 small jump rings

* 16in (41cm) of 28 gauge beading wire (silver-coloured)

* 2 large lace-end crimps

* 2 large jump rings

* 1 lobster clasp

* Needle and thread to match cotton cord

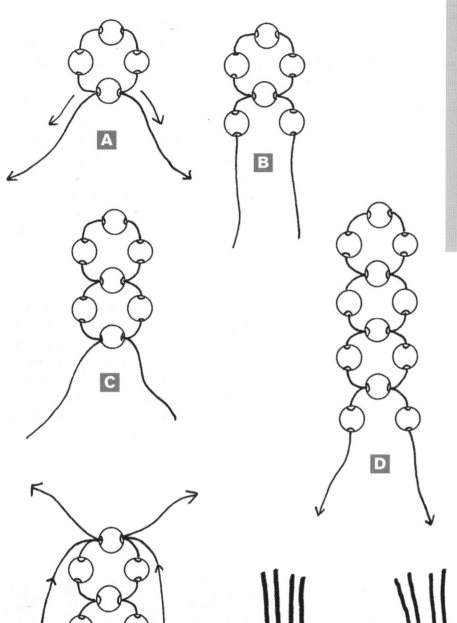

hints and tips

When using freshwater pearls, always be sure to check that the central holes are large enough to thread your head pins or wire through before starting your project.

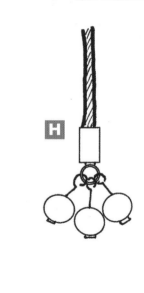

a dab of glue and fix one of the large lace-end crimps over the top (refer to **Leather and Cotton Thong**, page 25).

Step 6

Push the two folded ends of the cord together through the centre of one of the large-hole spacer beads and push the spacer up the cords about 2in (5cm) (**F**).

Step 7

Next thread the two folded ends through the centre of the pearl cluster you made in steps **A** to **E** (end to end) and then through the second large-hole spacer bead. Push up the cords to meet the other spacer bead (**G**).

Step 8

Next attach the four shorter lengths of cotton cord together at one end, having all four ends even. Attach the ends together by binding or stitching them with thread, then add a dab of glue and fix one of the large lace-end crimps over the top (refer to, **Leather and Cotton Thong**, page 25).

Step 9

Stagger the cut ends slightly so that all four lengths are uneven, and then attach a small lace-end crimp to the end of each length of cord.

Step 10

Thread a pearl onto each of 12 of the short head pins, turn a loop at the top (refer to **Making a Loop in Wire**, page 17) then attach three head pin pearl dangles to each of four of the small jump rings. Attach each jump ring to one of the small lace-end crimps – there will now be three pearls dangling in a group on each of the four lengths (**H**).

Step 11

Next attach the lobster clasp to one of the large lace-end crimps using one large jump ring. At the other end attach the other large jump ring and join the remaining three small jump rings together in a chain. Make a dangle with the remaining two pearls and short head pin and attach this to the bottom of the small jump ring chain. Do the necklace up at the clasp (back).

Step 12

Finally, open up the folded end cotton cord loop on the first half of the necklace, thread the four tails with the pearl ends through the loop then push the spacer bead, pearl cluster and other spacer bead together up tight against the folded loop.

variations

This necklace would take on a completely different look made from **tan** or **natural cotton cord** paired with some of the wonderful **bronze** or **brown** tone **freshwater pearls** currently available. Try using cream-coloured pearls with the black for a **monochromatic** look.

ida

SHORT ASYMMETRIC NECKLACE

The 1940s asymmetric styling of this necklace is deceptively simple because it can be made in a multitude of colour and bead choices from vintage glass flowers to contemporary plain resin for a whole host of different looks. It is one of the most popular necklaces that I have made and sold over the years.

Using classy bronze clay beads gives a refined and elegant look – incorporating the tiny glass flowers in the 'branches' at the front gives a more delicate and feminine appearance. Try using larger vintage beads on the branches for a more striking look or find an individual hand-blown glass bead to create a special focal point.

you will need

* Approx 45in (115cm) of tiger tail wire
* 120 approx short bugle beads (6mm length)
* 8 x 4mm glass pearls
* 2 glass flower beads (drilled top to bottom)
* 1 large feature bead (15 x 20mm approx) with a central hole large enough to take 3 strands of tiger tail together
* 7 or 8 crimp beads
* 2 clam shell calottes
* 1 bolt ring clasp
* 6 jump rings
* 1 glass leaf bead

making up instructions

hints and tips

The materials listed here will make a necklace that is approximately 15in (38cm) long. If you want a longer necklace, add a few more bugles to each of the three strands and a few to the end of the single strand.

If you use longer bugle beads, you will have to adjust the number of beads you use. The beads used in this project are 6mm bugles.

Step 1

Cut the tiger tail wire into three pieces; one length of 19in (49cm) and two lengths of 13in (33cm). Thread all three wires through the calotte and a crimp bead with ends even. Squash the crimp securing all three wires together, trim the tails close to the calotte add a drop of glue then close the calotte over the top of the crimp (refer to, **Using End Findings**, page 16).

Step 2

Then on each of the three wires, thread 29 bugle beads (refer to step **A** throughout for stringing).

Step 3

Take all three wires together through the large feature bead (**B**).

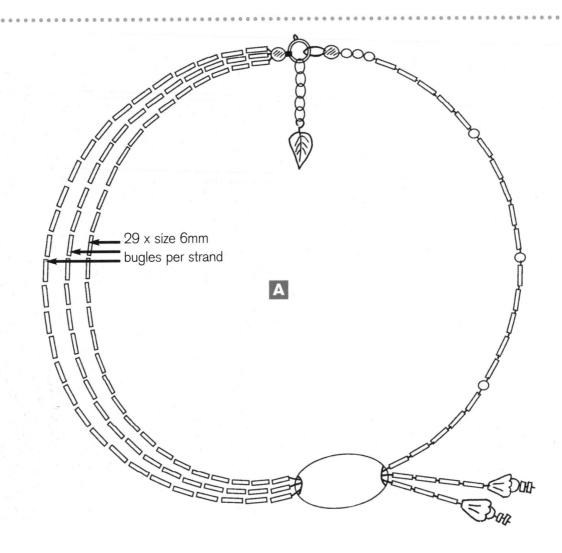

29 x size 6mm
bugles per strand

A

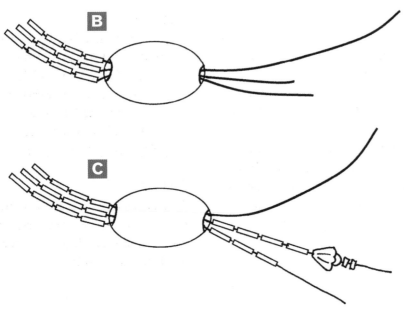

B

C

Step 4

On one short wire tail, thread four bugles, a glass flower bead, a 4mm glass pearl bead then a crimp. Adjust the tension on the strand so that it will hang correctly (not too tight) and squash the crimp to secure the beads in place. Add another crimp and squash it close against the first for security.

Step 5

On the other short tail, thread three bugles, a glass flower bead, a 4mm glass pearl bead then a crimp. Adjust the tension on the

The plain **olive green** and **bronze** version of the necklace (pictured right) uses size 7mm bugles, 24 on each of the three strands, and just four bugles between beads on the single strand.

The matching **bracelet** is made in the same way as the necklace, but for the long single strand I have used **26 gauge** beading wire, with **tiger tail** for just the two shorter lengths. This is so that the bracelet can be bent into shape more easily. The bracelet uses eight size 7mm bugles for each of the three strands and alternate bugles and oval beads (total of six bugles) for the single strand. On the 'sprigs' there are just two bugles on the first and three on the second.

You could also make a pair of matching **earrings** along the same lines as those in **Marilyn**, page 128.

strand so that it will hang correctly and squash the crimp to secure the beads in place. Add another crimp and squash it close against the first for security (**C**).

Step 6
Next take the long strand. Thread on five bugles then a 4mm glass pearl. Thread on another five bugles then another 4mm glass pearl bead. Thread on five bugles then another 4mm glass pearl bead. Finally, thread on another five bugles and finish with three 4mm glass pearl beads.

Step 7
Take the wire tail through a calotte and thread on two crimp beads (for security). Push the crimps inside the calotte, adjusting the tension of the necklace so that it hangs correctly, then squash the crimps to secure in place. Trim tail of wire; add a drop of glue inside the calotte, then close the calotte over the crimps (refer to **Using End Findings**, page 16).

Step 8
Attach the bolt ring fastener to one of the calottes using one of the jump rings. At the other end, join four of the jump rings together in a chain and attach to the calotte. Attach the leaf bead to the four jump rings using the final jump ring.

Step 9
Trim the tails of the front branches of the necklace close to the crimps once you are sure they are secure and hanging correctly.

bobby

ORGANDIE RIBBON HEART NECKLACE

This delicate and feminine necklace is made using an Indian glass heart pendant as a focal point, which although modern and inexpensive is evocative of a more romantic era.

In keeping with the 1940s design ethic, Bobby uses economical and inventive materials, combining reasonably priced pretty organza ribbon with soft knotted cotton cord.

The cord and ribbon are held together with decorative metal spacer beads and the knots keep these in place. A dainty glass heart on the clasp adds extra interest at the neckline.

making up instructions

hints and tips

The materials listed (right) will make a necklace that is 15in (38cm) in length.

This is a short necklace designed so that the pendant can be seen high in the neckline. The ribbon and cord combination sits better and is therefore better suited to shorter length necklaces. However, if you wanted to make a slightly shorter or longer necklace you could vary the distances between the knots – maybe leaving 1¾in (45mm) between each block instead of 1½in (38mm).

Step 1
At one end of the cotton cord, add a dab of glue and with cut ends even wrap the ribbon around the cord and attach the lace-end crimp over the ribbon/cord, fastening them together (refer to **Leather and Cotton Thong**, page 25) (**A**).

Step 2
Thread the other end of the ribbon through the needle. Then approximately 1½in (38mm) from the lace end, tie an overhand knot in the cotton cord (**B**).

Step 3
Next thread the needle with the ribbon through a metal spacer bead, then thread the end of the cotton cord through the metal spacer bead as well. Push the bead up against the knot in the cord and pull the ribbon so that it is of equal length to the cord. Now tie another overhand knot in the cotton cord tight up

you will need

* 30in (76cm) of 1mm cotton cord or leather thong
* 18in (46cm) of ¼in (6mm) organza ribbon
* 8 metal spacer beads with large central holes
* 2 large lace-end crimps
* 5 jump rings
* 1 bolt ring clasp
* Large decorative glass or metal heart pendant
* Small glass heart pendant (for back dangle)
* Needle/bodkin with large eye and blunt end

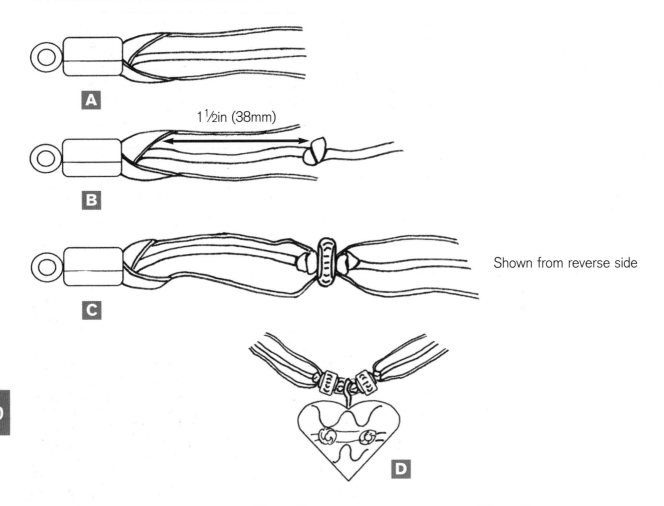

A

B

1½in (38mm)

C

Shown from reverse side

D

against the other side of the metal spacer bead (**C**).

Step 4

Repeat this process by making another knot in the cord approximately 1½in (38mm) from the last knot; thread the needle with the ribbon through a metal spacer bead, then thread the end of the cotton cord through the metal spacer bead as well. Push the bead up against the knot in the cord and pull the ribbon so that it is of equal length to the cord. Now tie another overhand knot in the cotton cord tight up against the other side of the metal spacer bead.

Step 5

Make two more knot/spacer/knot blocks approximately 1½in (38mm) apart so that you have a total of four spacers threaded.

Step 6

Directly after the last knot, thread on the large glass heart pendant (either directly hanging by the loop at the top or via a jump ring). Thread both the cotton cord and the ribbon through the pendant loop, then tie another overhand knot in the cotton cord directly after the pendant.

Step 7

Next thread the needle with the ribbon through a metal spacer bead, then thread the end of the cotton cord through the metal spacer bead as well. Push the bead up against the last knot in the cord and pull the ribbon so that it is of equal length to the cord. Now tie another overhand knot in the cotton cord tight up against the other side of the metal spacer bead. The pendant will now sit snugly between two knot/spacer/ knot blocks at the front, which will stop it from moving around (**D**).

Step 8

Make three more knot/spacer/knot blocks approximately 1½in (38mm) apart so that you have a total of four blocks on this side of the pendant to match the first.

Step 9

From the last knot, measure 1½in (38mm), ensure that the ribbon is not puckered and cut the ribbon and cotton cord so that they are 1½in (38mm) in length. Add a dab of glue to the cotton cord and with the cut ends even wrap the ribbon around the cord and attach the second lace-end crimp over the ribbon/cord, fastening them together (refer to **Leather and Cotton Thong**, page 25).

Step 10

At one end attach the bolt ring fastener using one of the jump rings. At the other end join the remaining four jump rings together in a chain and attach the small glass heart to the bottom jump ring.

variations

For a less heavy centrepiece, there are a variety of **cast metal** pendants on the market from which to suspend beads, or you could make a heart using **wire** and **beads**. The wired heart used on the cuff in **Rhonda**, page 140, could be used as a pendant or you could make one on a **wire jig** and wrap it with fine gauge wire and beads.

The **clear glass** heart necklace (pictured below) uses a special metal bead with a large centre hole, and a loop from which I have hung the pendant as a variation.

dolores

VINTAGE BUTTON TIE CHOKER

This project has the simple utilitarian feel of the 1940s but with a touch of glamour in the festoons and Swarovski crystal drops.

Dolores offers a great way to combine soft, plain ribbon with delicate seed beads to highlight the genuine antique or vintage buttons. It is uncomplicated, especially made in the black but is very effective for evening wear or even with a tea dress for garden parties. As it only needs very few focal buttons it presents a great way of using up odd vintage buttons or short lengths of antique ribbon – in the true tradition of 1940s make-do-and-mend.

you will need

* 12in (30.5cm) of velvet ribbon ⅝in (16mm) wide
* 12in (30.5cm) of satin or grosgrain ribbon for backing, same width or slightly narrower than the velvet ribbon
* 26in (66cm) of satin ribbon for ties ⅛in (3mm) wide
* 3 vintage buttons (at least 2 the same)
* 2 Swarovski crystal teardrop-shaped beads (top drilled)
* 2 Swarovski crystal 4mm faceted beads
* Approx 60 size 10 seed beads (regular sizes are best)
* Beading needle threaded with 40in (1m) of nylon beading thread (Nymo is best)
* Sewing thread to match ribbon

making up instructions

Step 1
Cut the narrow ribbon in half and stitch a piece to the velvet ribbon at each end. It should be positioned centrally on the right side of the velvet ribbon with cut ends even (**A**).

Step 2
Pin the backing ribbon to the velvet ribbon, right sides together and with the satin ties sandwiched in between in the seams (**B**). Machine stitch at either end down cut ends.

Step 3
Turn velvet ribbon right side out, pin backing ribbon to velvet ribbon at intervals and machine stitch together down both selvedge edges using a short machine stitch. Iron from the reverse side to even out any puckers (**C**).

Step 4
Angle the ends of the ties and add a dab of glue or fray-check to the ends to stop them from fraying.

Step 5
Find the centre of the choker and put a pin in vertically. Stitch one of the vintage buttons in the centre. If you have one which is more of a 'centrepiece' use this in the middle.

Step 6
Next measure to points 1½in (4cm) from either side of the centre button. Mark the points with a vertical pin then stitch a vintage button at this point on either side. I have used buttons with two centre holes. When you have stitched the button on with about three stitches, take the needle up through the first hole then through one of the 4mm

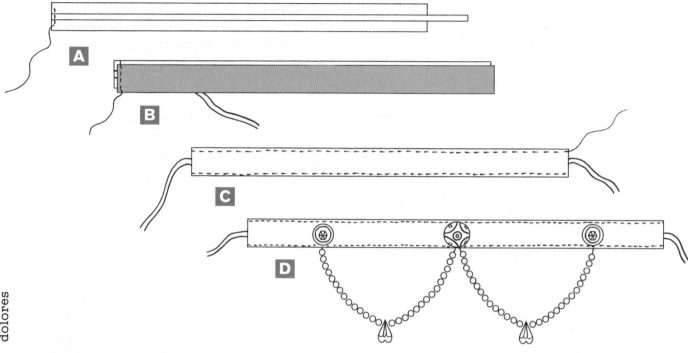

Swarovski beads and back down through the second hole in the button. Repeat this three times. Do the same for the button on the other side. **NB: It helps to use a button with a dent on the top surface, in which the bead can sit.**

Step 7
Now make the festoons (**D**). Thread the beading needle with the beading thread so that it is double and with ends even tie a knot. Take the needle into the velvet ribbon underneath one vintage button on one side of the choker. Make a couple of stitches to ensure that the thread is secure in the ribbon, then take the needle/thread down and out between the velvet and backing ribbon, directly underneath the vintage button.

Step 8
On the needle pick up 14 or 15 seed beads then thread on one Swarovski crystal teardrop bead and a further 14 or 15 seed beads.

Step 9
Next take the needle/thread up between the velvet and backing ribbon directly underneath the centre vintage button. Make a couple of stitches up underneath the button to secure the thread then take the needle/thread back down between the velvet and backing ribbon directly next to the point where you came up, underneath the centre vintage button.

Step 10
On the needle pick up 14 or 15 seed beads then thread on the other Swarovski crystal teardrop bead and a further 14 or 15 seed beads.

Step 11
Next take the needle/thread up between the velvet and backing ribbon directly underneath the third vintage button. Make a couple of stitches up underneath the button to secure the thread underneath the third button.

Step 12
At this point if you wish you can take the thread back through all of the beads a second time by retracing your steps back in the opposite direction. If you are using a strong thread like Nymo, this should not be necessary. Although doubling up adds extra security you do not want the bead festoons to hang too stiffly.

You could use any pretty **vintage** or **glass buttons** for this project. If you preferred you could use five small buttons or you could make four **overlapping festoons** instead of two to create a more dramatic or decorative piece (see the **antique beige choker** pictured left).

You could also utilize very **plain** tiny vintage buttons paired with **ornamental** hand-painted **scalloped lace** and narrower velvet ribbon (such as the **lilac and grey** lace choker pictured right). The possibilities are endless.

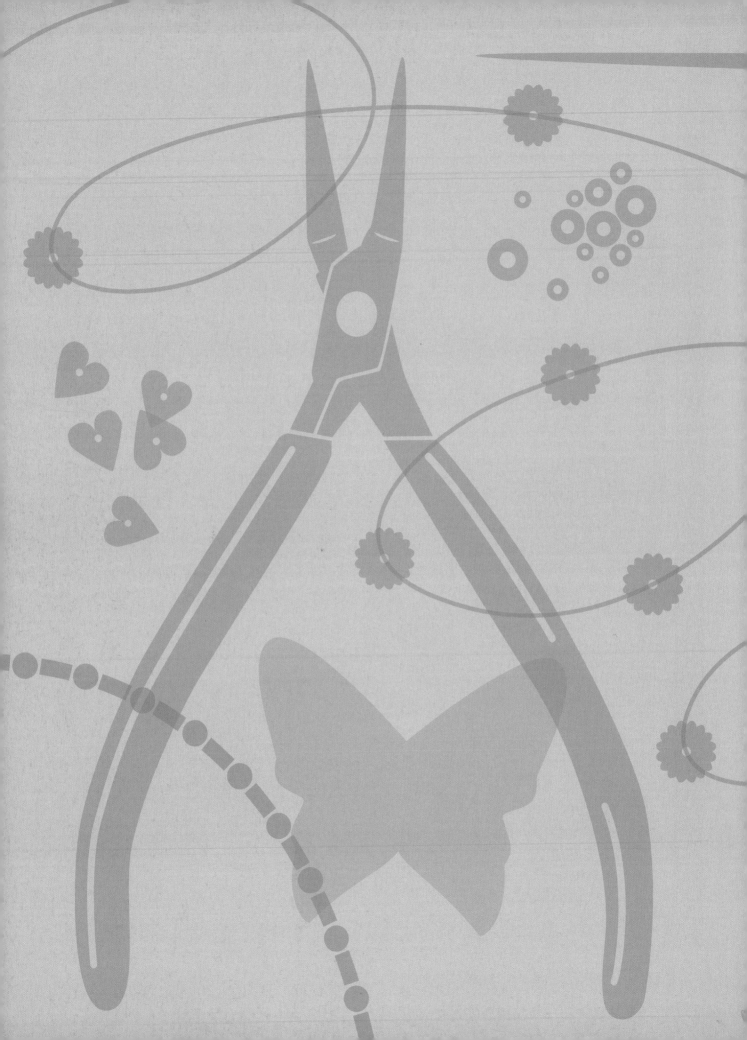

1950s

marilyn

ROSE PEARL CUFF

This pretty cuff combines the feminine 1950s charm of ribbon roses and leaves with clusters of delightful freshwater pearls, also popular in this decade.

The cuff could be worn to its best advantage with a 50s style elbow-length cashmere cardigan or would be equally stunning worn with a sleeveless dress for a wedding or summer party. Make the project in fresh spring lilacs paired with sterling silver wire as I have or give it a completely different appeal in autumnal bronzes and rusts with gold-plated wire. You could also use colour-coated wire to create a less precious look.

you will need

* 50in (127cm) of 26 gauge non-tarnish beading wire
* 24 freshwater pearls (colour 1)
* 12 freshwater pearls (colour 2)
* 3 ribbon roses, approx ¾in (19mm) diameter
* 4½in (11.5cm) of ¾in (19mm) wide organdie ribbon for leaf
* 2 crimps
* 2 clam shell calottes
* 7 medium-sized jump rings
* 1 bolt ring fastener
* 1 small head pin
* 2 pearls for the dangle
* Thread to match roses/ribbon and a needle

making up instructions

Step 1
First find the centre of the length of wire and loosely fold it in half. Thread a crimp on to the wire and push it to the centre fold. Next with both ends of the wire even, take them through the hole in a clam shell calotte. Push the calotte so that the crimp on the fold in the wire is inside the calotte. Close the calotte over the crimp (**A**).

Step 2
Twist the two wires together to create a central stem of around ½in (13mm) – be careful not to 'over twist' the wire because it may break and you will be unable to work a new piece into this design (**B**).

Step 3
Next separate the two wires. On one wire thread on three of the colour one pearls, with the centre pearl about ¾in (19mm) from where the wires meet (**C**). Twist the wire around on itself under the pearls to form a stem around ½in (13mm) long. Do the same with three pearls and the wire on the opposite side.

Step 4
Twist the two wires together again to form a central stem around ⅜in (1cm) long. Then on the top wire pick up one of the colour two pearls and on the lower wire pick up two of the colour 2 pearls. Place them so that the top pearl sits in between the lower two (**D**). Twist the wires together after the cluster to form a central stem of around ⅜in (1cm).

Step 5
Leave a slight gap of around ⅛in (3mm) on each wire then pick up three colour 1 pearls on each strand and twist ½in (13mm) stems as in step **C**. At the base of each

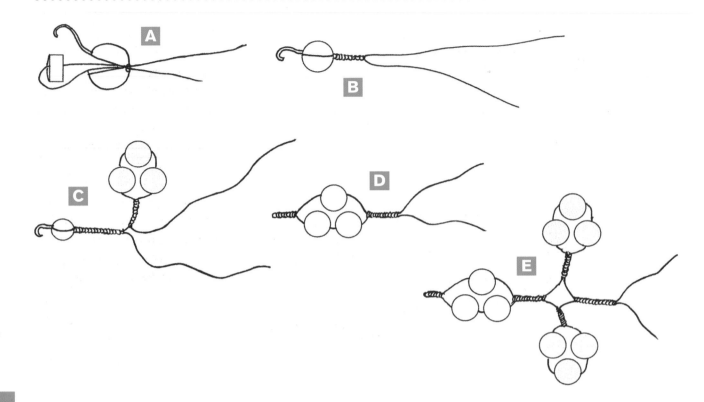

stem leave a gap of around ⅛in (3mm) then twist the wires together to create a central stem of around ⅜in (9mm). This will leave a small diamond-shaped gap in the wire to which you will eventually stitch the first of the ribbon roses (**E**).

Step 6

Next on the top wire pick up one of the colour 2 pearls and on the lower wire pick up two of the colour 2 pearls, as in step **D**. Place them so that the top pearl sits in between the lower two, as in step **D**. Twist the wires together after the cluster to form a central stem of around ¼in (6mm).

Step 7

Next, leave a gap of around ½in (13mm) then twist the wires together again to form another

¼in (6mm) stem the other side of the gap. The gap will be opened out into a diamond shape where you will eventually stitch the central ribbon leaf and rose.

Step 8

Complete the second half of the cuff as a mirror image of the first with two more central clusters of three pearls and four more branches of three pearls on the sides. After the last two side branches, twist the wires together to form a central stem of about ½in (13mm).

Step 9

Thread the tails of both wires through the central hole in the other clam shell calotte, thread them both through a crimp, and push the crimp and calotte to

where the twisting ends. Next squash the crimp, cut the wires back to within ¼in (6mm) and fold the wire ends over the crimp using pliers. Close the calotte over the crimp.

Step 10

Attach the clasp to one calotte using one of the jump rings. Attach the remaining six jump rings together in a chain and attach this to the other calotte. Make a head-pin dangle using the final two pearls and attach this to the bottom jump ring in the chain (refer to **Making a Loop in Wire**, page 17).

Step 11

Open out the diamond shapes in the wire and stitch the two side ribbon roses to the cuff. Place the

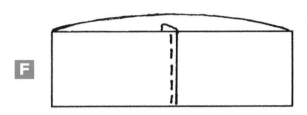

F

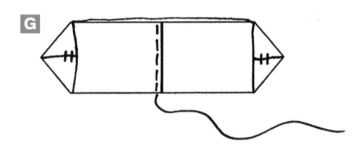

G

It is often hard to get bracelets or cuffs the right size and most people overestimate the size needed. This bracelet should measure 6¼in (16cm) before you attach the clasp and jump rings. You can always add extra jump rings or an extender chain to make the bracelet larger. However, it is not possible to make it smaller if you start off with it too large.

centre of the rose in the diamond, and with the rose on the right side stitch from the reverse over all four supporting wires.

Step 12

Make the leaf by folding the ribbon with both cut ends towards the centre. Fold under a hem and pin in place. Fold the folded corners of the ribbon inward to form a point at each end of the leaf and stitch in place (see the petals in **Ruby**, page 100, for more help with this). Gather stitch up the folded hemmed centre of the ribbon and pull up, securing gathers with a few stitches (**F G**).

Step 13

Stitch the final rose onto the centre of the ribbon leaf with the join in the leaf facing downwards. Open

the gap in the centre of the cuff into a diamond shape and stitch the leaf and flower to all four wires from the reverse side.

Step 14

Finally, bend the outer pearl branches forwards towards the central rose and shape the cuff around the wrist.

variations

There are a number of purchased **ribbon flowers** on the market which you could use for this project. You could always try **hand-painting** the flowers with fabric dye as in **Rosaline**, page 93, for a more antiqued look. If you don't want such a large focal ribbon leaf in the centre, you could use several strands of **fine ribbon** and leave them hanging a little longer for a totally different appearance.

lori

CHAIN CHARM EARRINGS

Fringes were a popular feature of 1950s jewellery and these earrings offer a contemporary take on this theme. Charm earrings and necklaces are enjoying a revival in current fashion.

you will need

* ✱ 16 links of trace chain (medium-sized) – 8 links for each earring

* ✱ 16 small head pins – 8 per earring, one for each chain link

* ✱ 1 pair of earring wires

* ✱ 6 semi-precious stone chips or freshwater pearls in pale pink (holes large enough to thread a small head pin through)

* ✱ 10 large (size 6) seed beads, clear glass

* ✱ 10 x 4mm cream pearls or faceted

* ✱ 4 bugle beads, silver or clear

* ✱ 4 glass cushion-shaped beads in pink

These earrings are wonderfully versatile because they can be made using any odd beads you have left over, in toning shades – as long as you have enough to make a matching pair! These were made using a mixture of glass pearls, semi-precious stone chips, large seed beads and bugles. The chain makes a good base for the 'charms' as it has movement, but is still very secure. Once you have grasped the technique of making 'loops' in head pins you will find yourself making these earrings to match every outfit!

making up instructions

Step 1
Begin by cutting the chain (with heavy wire cutters or by opening the links) into two lengths, each with eight chain links.

Step 2
Attach each length of chain to an earring wire at one end of the chain.

Step 3
Make the head pin 'charm' dangles in pairs so that you are sure you have the same for both earrings. Make dangles by threading appropriate beads onto the head pins and turning a loop above the beads (refer to **Making a Loop in Wire**, page 17).

Step 4
Attach only one dangle to each link of each chain for this particular pair of earrings (refer to the diagram on page 134 to see the threading pattern of the charms).

Step 5
Attach charm dangles by opening and closing the loop at the top of the head pin from side to side as you would a jump ring. The process is fiddly but well worth the effort.

Step 6
Make the two earrings at the same time, attaching the charm dangles to each earring in the same link order so that you are sure you have a matching pair.

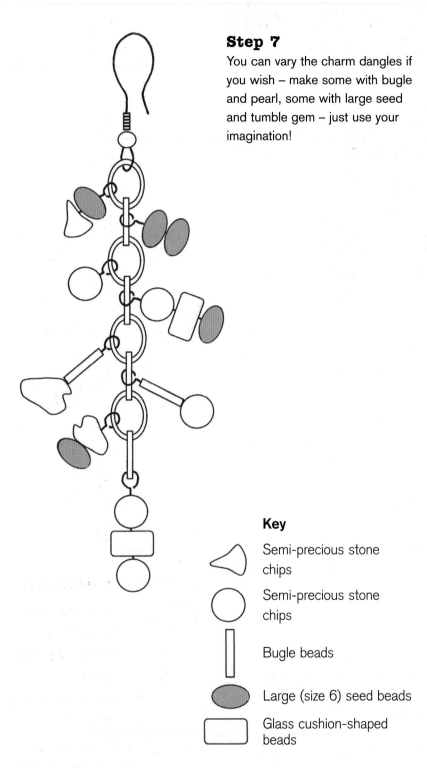

lori

1950s

Step 7

You can vary the charm dangles if you wish – make some with bugle and pearl, some with large seed and tumble gem – just use your imagination!

Key

◁	Semi-precious stone chips
○	Semi-precious stone chips
▯	Bugle beads
⬭	Large (size 6) seed beads
▭	Glass cushion-shaped beads

The two pairs of earrings pictured above and right are made using the same technique as the pink ones, but instead of using a pre-made chain as a base I have linked eight small jump rings together to form a chain for each earring.

For each earring in the bronze leaf pair, make three head pin dangles, each with a copper glass pearl and a black 4mm faceted glass bead, and attach a small jump ring to the top of each of three bronze top-drilled leaves.

On the bottom jump ring hang a pressed glass black leaf and then join two more jump rings above this one.

On the fourth jump ring in the chain, hang a bead dangle one side and a bronze leaf the other, both on the same jump ring link.

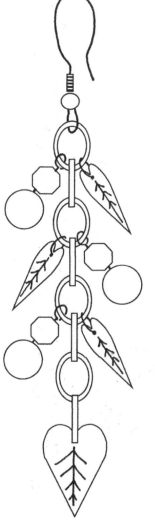

▲ These wonderful 50s-inspired bright gold, red and green earrings and the bronze leaf pair are both made along the same lines, using jump rings instead of pre-made chain.

Key for bronze leaf earrings

Bronze leaf bead on jump ring

Bronze 6mm glass pearl bead

Black 4mm faceted glass bead

Black pressed glass vintage leaf

Join one plain (fifth) jump ring and on the sixth jump ring hang a bronze leaf and a bead dangle, both on the same ring again but this time on opposite sides to the previous two.

Attach one more jump ring in between then finish at the top by hanging the final bead dangle and

bronze leaf, again on opposite sides of the eighth jump ring, then attach this ring directly to the loop of the earring wire.

Using jump rings allows you to open the rings and build a 'chain' as you go. It is essential though to build both earrings as you go to make sure you get a pair.

making **vintage** jewellery

evangeline

RIBBON TRIM GARLAND NECKLACE

This pretty necklace is evocative of childhood daisy chains, the fine wire barely visible between the 'floating' beads and the soft silk ribbon bows. It has all the feminine allure of 1950s fashions but uses opulent semi-precious beads and pearls to create a 'cobbled together' contemporary look.

Evangeline would look equally at home with a diaphanous summer dress or gracing the neckline of a soft sweater or silk shirt. The possibilities with this design are endless. Make it up in starkly contrasting black and cream or in pastel floral colours for early summer picnics and lazy garden parties. With careful toning it will complement any outfit.

making up instructions

hints and tips

The materials listed (right) will make a necklace that is approximately 15in (38cm) in length.

These instructions are based on making a six strand necklace. Quantities for four to eight strands should be adjusted accordingly

Step 1

Start by taking all three of the 58in (150cm) wires together through the hole in the lobster clasp. Find the centre of the wires and fold the wires in half over the clasp so that you have six equal length pieces of wire to work with. Then thread all six wires through one of the large seed beads (check that the hole is big enough) and a large crimp. Push them up fairly close against the clasp and squash the crimp (**A**).

Step 2

Work one strand at a time and thread one kind of bead only on each strand. Begin by threading on a pearl bead, then making a loose knot in the wire next to it. (Refer to **Working with Fine Gauge Wire**, page 22.) Thread on another pearl

you will need

* 174in (450cm) of 28 gauge wire, cut into 3 lengths of 58in (150cm) each (the wire used for the mauve tone necklace has a lilac-coloured finish)

* 11 medium-sized freshwater pearls in lilac

* 11 medium-sized freshwater pearls in sage green

* 11 semi-precious stone chips (drilled)

* 26 large (size 6) clear pink seed beads

* 24 two-tone effect large (size 6) seed beads

* Approx 40in (1m) of silk ribbon, ½in (13mm) width

* 1 medium or large-sized lobster clasp

* 1 solid jump ring

* 2 large crimps

* 5 ordinary large jump rings

* 1 head pin

* Extra seed beads, pearls or chips for the dangle

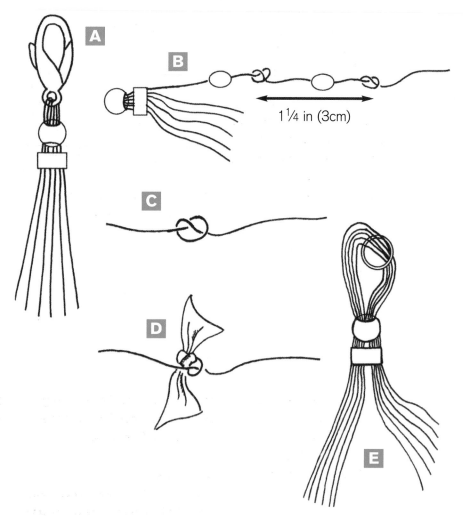

bead and make another knot. There should be roughly 10 or 11 knots per strand, and 10 or 11 beads per strand to make a close fitting necklace of approximately 15in (38cm). The knots will be approximately 1¼in (3cm) apart with the beads floating loose in between (**B**).

Step 3

Continue until you have reached the desired length with the first strand. You can then make the other strands the same length. It should measure around 13in (33cm) from the first large crimp to the last knot. The wire tails at that end and the clasp will add around 2in (5cm).

1¼ in (3cm)

For a different appearance, try using narrow ½in (13mm) **satin ribbon** for the ties and finish the ends with fray-check – the **rust and brown** version of the necklace (left) has been made in this way.

You could also use either inexpensive **glass beads** for a more casual look or non-tarnish **sterling silver wire** for a more precious piece. Incorporate **vintage glass flowers** or **leaves** to accentuate the feminine side.

Step 4

Always finish each strand with a knot to prevent the beads from falling off as you work the other strands. You can always add a bead onto the end of the strands before finishing the necklace off if you feel it is necessary.

Step 5

Work five of the strands with the beads. Thread one strand with each of the pearl colours, one strand with the stone chips and on two strands thread two large seed beads in between each knot (one strand with each colour of seed beads). They should all be the same length as your first strand.

Step 6

On the sixth strand, tie knots only – do not thread any beads in between (**C**). Keep the knots fairly open and rounded. When you have finished the knots, thread a length of silk ribbon (approximately 3½in (9cm) long) through each wire knot and tie a tight overhand knot in the ribbon. Cut the ribbon tails back to around ½in (13mm) with the ends at an angle to minimize fraying (**D**). **NB: If you don't want the ribbon to fray at all, you can dab the ends with Fray Check. However, a little fraying adds to the softness of the piece if using silk ribbon.**

Step 7

When you have finished the last strand, thread all six strands together through a large (size 6) seed bead, then through a large

The loop on a lobster clasp is 'solid' so none of the wires can escape through a gap. This is also the reason for using a solid ring at the other end of the necklace.

Keep the wire in large 'rounded' loops as you make the knots. Work on one strand at a time and take your time with the knots. Keep your index finger in the loop until you are sure that the knot is in the right place. Then gently tighten the loop into a loose knot. Be careful not to get kinks or sharp bends in the wire as this will make it more likely to break. If the wire breaks in this design, you will not be able to rectify it by working in a new piece.

crimp and then through the solid jump ring. Take all wires back through the crimp, and then back through the bead if possible. You can now see why you need beads with large holes!

Step 8

Pull the strands up fairly tight to form a loop over the jump ring and push the crimp and bead up against it. You will need to pull the wires very carefully and one at a time to form the tight loop and ensure that the wire does not break (**E**). (Also refer to **Finishing Off With Fine Wire**, page 23).

Step 9

Squash the crimp carefully, and then wrap all six tails of wire around the crimp and the supporting strands about four times. Then cut off the tails of four

strands and wrap the remaining two strands around several times to cover the four ends.

Step 10

With the final two tails, wrap these around all strands close up beside the large seed bead. Clip the tails and hide against the bead.

Step 11

Finally, join the five jump rings together in a chain and join this to the solid jump ring. Make a dangle by threading a mixture of pearls, chips and seed beads onto a head pin and turning a loop above them (refer to **Making a Loop in Wire**, page 17). Attach this to the bottom jump ring in the chain. The chain of jump rings will be used to fasten the necklace and will allow for any variation in size.

139

rhonda

PLEATED HEART CUFF

Witty, figurative motifs including heart shapes, cartoon animals, fruit and flowers were popular in 1950s fashions. This cuff uses Victorian style ribbon work to create a pleated grosgrain ribbon base for the glass beaded heart centrepiece. The tiny beads trimming the ribbon pleats tie in with the heart.

This is a fancy, decorative piece that could easily be translated into a choker by increasing the number of pleats and the length of the ribbon. The cuff would make a softer alternative to a bracelet with summer wear and would be ideally paired with a three-quarter-length sleeved cardigan or jacket, or a short-sleeved blouse. It would also be perfect for evening wear (see the black version) with a sleeveless dress.

you will need

* Approx 22in (56cm) of grosgrain ribbon in main colour ½in (13mm) width

* Approx 7in (18cm) of grosgrain ribbon in backing colour, ⅝in (16mm) width

* 15 x 4mm faceted beads

* Approx 23 x large seed beads (size 8 or 6)

* 35in (90cm) of 28 gauge beading wire (to tone with beads)

* 2 choker end plates

* Bolt ring or small lobster fastener

* 6 small jump rings

* 2 larger jump rings

* 1 short head pin

* 1 small heart-shaped glass bead for dangle

* Sewing thread to match ribbon and a needle

making up instructions

the bead heart

Step 1

Begin by making the beaded heart for the centre of the cuff. Pick up three 4mm beads and push them to the centre of the length of beading wire. Pick up a fourth 4mm bead then take both wire tails in opposite directions through the centre of it to form a circle (**A**).

Step 2

Pick up another two 4mm beads on the lower wire tail, then pick up a third 4mm bead and cross the tails of both wires in opposite directions through it (**B**). Pick up another two 4mm beads on the upper wire tail, then pick up a third 4mm bead and cross both wires through it with tails exiting in opposite directions (**C**).

Step 3

On the upward-pointing tail, thread on five large seed beads, then take the tail through the top centre right 4mm bead and top centre left 4mm bead. With the downward-pointing tail, pick up one seed bead and take the tail through the lower right 4mm bead (**D**).

Step 4

With the upper tail, pick up five large seed beads then take the tail down through the left central 4mm bead. With the lower tail, pick up one large seed bead and take the tail up through the lower left 4mm bead. Pick up another large seed bead then take the tail up through the left central 4mm bead. The two wire tails should now be exiting in opposite directions through this bead (**E**).

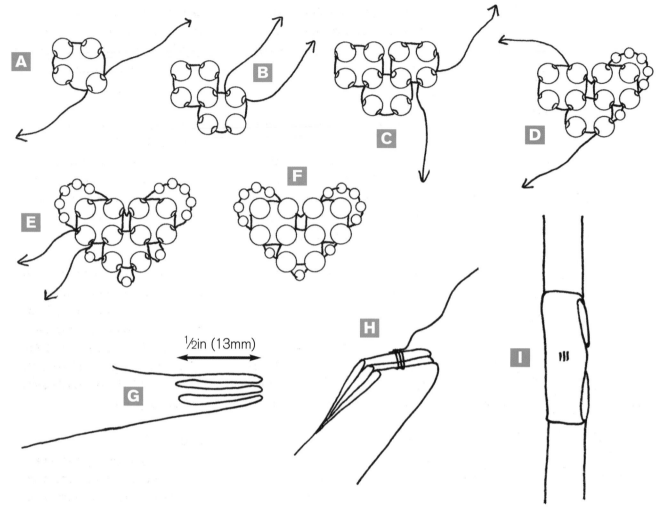

I have used **grosgrain** ribbon for this project because it is double-sided and is quite firm, making it easier to form sharp pleats. Any **double-faced ribbon** would suffice once you have got the hang of the technique – there are many double-sided **satin** and **organdie** ribbons on the market which would make pretty and alternative top layers.

Also consider using tiny **vintage buttons** on top of the pleats instead of the beads and using one **large decorative vintage button** as a centrepiece to replace the heart.

Step 5

Pull the wires up tight and if the holes in the beads are large enough, thread the wires back through adjacent beads, wrap the wires around the supporting wires on each side, then clip the tails and hide them inside a bead if possible (if not, just wrap the tails around the supporting wire, clip and make sure they are at the back of the piece when you stitch it to the cuff). The heart should look like diagram **F**. (Refer to **Finishing Off with Fine Wire**, page 23, for more help.)

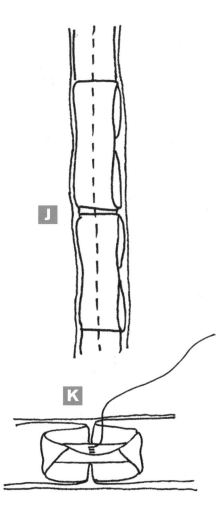

J

K

the ribbon cuff

Step 6

Take the longer length of grosgrain ribbon and make the first fold about 1½in (4cm) from one end. Fold the ribbon back towards the end, then fold it in the opposite direction to form a pleat. The pleat should be ½in (13mm) long. Fold the ribbon back towards the end of the ribbon again and then back in the opposite direction to form another pleat, ½in (13mm) long. Finally, fold the ribbon back towards the end again. Look at

diagram **G** – you should have three folds on the reverse of the ribbon and two folds on the inside of the ribbon.

Step 7

Holding the pleats firmly between finger and thumb with one hand, make three or four very small hand-stitches through all three pleats in the centre of the ribbon to hold them together (**H**). The stitches can go right through because they will be hidden inside the 'bow' formation and under the bead eventually.

Step 8

Now turn the ribbon over, right side up, and press the pleats open with your finger (**I**). Make two of these pleat formations right up against each other, then leave a 1in (25mm) gap (where you will eventually stitch the heart). Make a further two more pleat formations the other side of the gap.

Step 9

Machine stitch the pleated ribbon onto the backing grosgrain ribbon in a continuous line using short stitches (**J**). Stitch carefully down the centre of the pleats.

Step 10

Take the lower top layer of each box pleat and push it upwards and bring the upper top layer of each box pleat downward over the top of it. Hand-stitch in place with two to three stitches (**K**). After you have made two to three stitches, with the needle and thread in the

same place, pick up one seed bead, one 4mm bead and one seed bead, and then stitch in place over the previous stitches.

Step 11

Stitch the beaded heart in the centre of the cuff in the gap you left between pleats. Stitch using matching thread and sew around the supporting wires in between beads at both sides of the heart.

Step 12

For a cuff to fit a wrist between 6 and 7in (15 and 18cm) cut the ribbons back to ¼in (6mm) from the last pleat at each end of the cuff. Add glue to each end of the ribbon and attach end plates (refer to **Finishing Off Ribbon Chokers and Cuffs**, page 27).

Step 13

Join six jump rings together in a chain and attach to one end plate using one of the large jump rings. Make a dangle for the end of the chain by threading one seed bead, one 4mm bead and one seed bead onto the head pin. Turn a loop at the top (refer to **Making a Loop in Wire**, page 17). Attach to end jump ring in chain. Also attach small glass heart bead to end jump ring in chain. At the other end of the cuff join the clasp using the remaining large jump ring.

bridget

ROUNDED EVENING BAG WITH BEADED HANDLE AND DETACHABLE CORSAGE

This fabulous little O-shaped evening bag with its matching corsage is both decorative and versatile, being just large enough to carry the essentials.

Made from midnight purple cotton velvet with the elaborate floral trim and sumptuous striped silk lining, this bag would also be perfect for ladies' day at the races. The delicate beaded handle tones with the ribbons used to make the corsage, which is also trimmed with fronds fashioned from the same beads. You could even apply the technique used for the handle to make a flamboyant choker with the flower stitched to one side.

dimensions

The finished bag measures 7 x 7½in (18 x 19cm), excluding the handle

template

page 153

suggested fabrics

for main bag fabric:
Lightweight cotton velvet

for bag lining:
Firm weight silk

you will need

For the bag

✱ 12in (30cm) of cotton velvet (main fabric), 24in (61cm) wide

✱ 12in (30cm) of firm weight silk (lining fabric), 24in (61cm) wide

✱ 12in (30cm) of firm weight iron-on interfacing, 24in (61cm) wide

✱ Approx 16in (41cm) of velvet ribbon, ¼in (6mm) wide for handle loops and front trim

✱ 1 sew-on snap set

✱ Piece of plastic canvas to insert in base 5¼in x 1½in (13.5cm x 4cm)

For the handle

✱ Approx 50in (127cm) of tiger tail/flexible beading wire

✱ Approx 22 large (size 6) seed beads

✱ Approx 300 small seed beads (size 10/11)

✱ 2 medium/large crimp beads

cutting out

✱ Cut 2 x front/back from main fabric on fold

✱ Cut 2 x front/back from lining fabric on fold

✱ Cut 2 x front/back from iron-on interfacing on fold

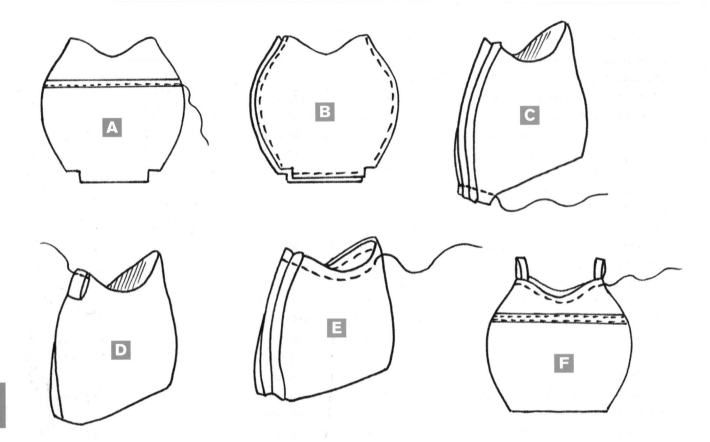

the bag

Step 1
Iron interfacing onto wrong side of front and back fabric sections following the manufacturer's guidelines.

Step 2
Pin the strip of velvet ribbon onto the front in position marked on pattern piece. Machine stitch in place along both edges of ribbon. Press lightly through a cloth from the back (**A**).

Step 3
Pin the two interfaced front/back pieces right sides of main fabric together. Stitch around sides and lower edges leaving corners free and leaving a ½in (13mm) seam allowance (**B**). Insert your finger into one of the bottom corners. Match up seams on bottom and side, pin through all thicknesses and stitch straight across the corner to form a gusset (**C**).

Step 4
Repeat this on the opposite corner. Clip into seam allowance at intervals along curved edge of bag. Turn bag right side out and press.

Step 5
Cut four pieces of narrow ribbon 2in (5cm) long. Stitch two pieces of ribbon together, wrong sides together down both sides to form a loop for the handle. Repeat this with the other two pieces of ribbon.

Step 6
On outside, positioned centred over side seams with raw edges even and loop facing downwards, pin handle loops to bag each side and baste in place (**D**).

Step 7
Stitch lining pieces together at sides and lower edges, leaving an opening of around 3½in (9cm) at centre of lower edge for turning. Form corners as for main bag.

Step 8

Insert bag into lining with right sides together. Pin lining to bag and baste together around upper edges. Pin and baste through all thicknesses, including handle loops, which will be sandwiched between the fabric and the lining. Machine stitch through all thicknesses using a medium stitch length and leaving a seam allowance of ½in (13mm). Ensure that you stitch slowly and carefully, especially over the handle loops. Trim the seam back to around ⅜in (1cm) to eliminate bulk. Clip carefully into seam allowance around curved edge (**E**).

Step 9

Turn the bag right side out through the opening in the bottom of the lining. Insert plastic canvas rectangle into base and then slip-stitch the opening closed. Turn the lining into the bag.

Step 10

Roll the lining with your fingers so that it is not visible from the outside, pin and hand-baste it in place around upper edge of bag. Top-stitch through all layers, about ¾in (19mm) from the top of the bag, using a medium stitch length and taking extra care when sewing through the bulkier areas (**F**). **NB: The bag is small and you need to top-stitch carefully**. Give the bag a light press. Hand-stitch the snap onto the lining on both sides at the point marked on the pattern piece.

the handle

Step 11

Refer to diagrams **G** to **I** for the handle. Start by threading the length of tiger tail wire through the handle carrier at one end and make sure that both ends of the wire are even.

Step 12

Thread 10 small seed beads onto each tail, then take both tails through a size 6 seed bead in opposite directions (**G**). This will form a circle. **NB: Four of the seed beads will then be inside the handle loop**. Next, on each tail thread six small seed beads, then take both tails through a size 6 seed bead in opposite directions. Continue threading each tail with six seed beads then taking the tails through a size 6 seed bead until you have threaded 22 size 6 seed beads (**H**).

Step 13

After the last (22nd) large (size 6) seed bead thread eight seed beads onto each tail. Take one tail through the handle carrier on the opposite side of the bag to where you started, making sure that the handle is not twisted. Thread two large crimp beads onto this tail, then take the other wire tail through the crimp in the opposite direction (**I**). Feed the tails back through a few beads, then pull the wires up so that the beads are snug against each other. Adjust the tension so that the handle is not

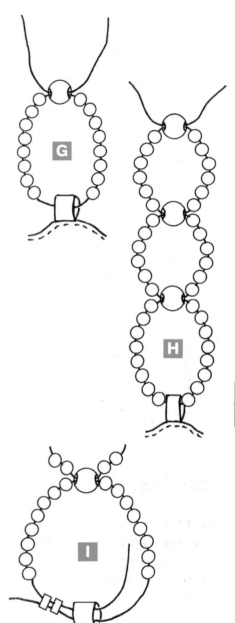

too stiff, then squash the crimps firmly. **NB: Ensure that the crimps are secure as the handle must be strong enough to take the weight of the bag**. Cut the tails of the wire back and hide inside the beads. The crimps should be inside the ribbon handle carrier.

the beaded corsage

you will need

* 1 ribbon flower (approx 2in (5cm) diameter)

* Approx 10in (25cm) of ⅝in (16mm) velvet ribbon (to match narrow ribbon trim on bag)

* Approx 10in (25cm) of 1in (25mm) toning organdie ribbon

* 1 brooch backing bar (with holes for sewing)

* Approx 10 large (size 6) seed beads

* Approx 200 small seed beads (size 10/11)

* Nymo beading thread and a beading needle

Step 1

Fold the velvet ribbon right side out in a figure-of-eight pattern, referring to diagrams **A** and **B** to form the leaves. Secure folds in place with a few hand stitches. Repeat this with the organdie ribbon, making sure the raw edges are hidden on the top side, which will be covered by the flower.

Step 2

Layer the leaves on top of each other at a slight angle, with the velvet on top so that you can see the organdie ribbon underneath. Hand-stitch the leaves together at the sides and then stitch the ribbon flower on top of the leaf base, along both outside edges. Stitch a brooch backing bar to the reverse of the leaves towards the top.

▲ You could make this corsage on its own to wear as a brooch on a jacket lapel or cardigan.

Step 3

To make the beaded fringe, thread the needle with a length of Nymo which is about 40in (1m) in length when doubled. Tie the cut ends together in an overhand knot, take the needle in underneath the flower and attach the thread to the leaf base about ¼in (6mm) left of the centre, with a few stitches.

Step 4

Pick up about 12 small seed beads, then pick up a further four. Pick up three seed beads, then one large seed bead and three further small seed beads. Now take the needle back up the previous four small seed beads in the opposite direction, taking care not to split the thread and pull up tight to form a loop (**C**). Pick up another four small seed beads, then a group of three small seeds, one large seed and three small seeds. Then take the needle back up the previous four small seed beads in the opposite direction and pull up tight to form a loop. Next take the needle back up the original 12 seed beads in the opposite direction (**D**) until you reach the leaf base again. Pull up tight (but allow for hanging space) and secure with a few stitches in the leaf base.

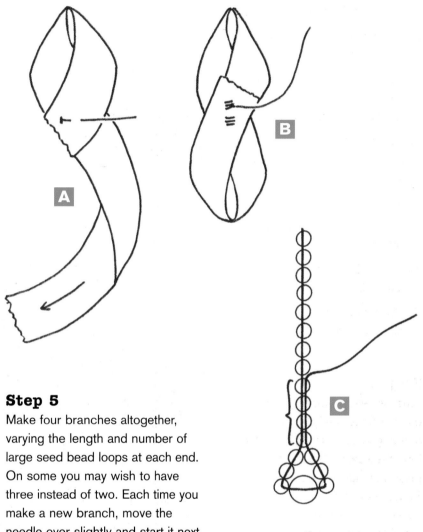

Step 5

Make four branches altogether, varying the length and number of large seed bead loops at each end. On some you may wish to have three instead of two. Each time you make a new branch, move the needle over slightly and start it next to the previous one on the leaf base, so that they will hang correctly. Finish off by making several stitches into the base to secure and snip the thread. Attach the corsage to the bag on the left-hand side, positioned over the strip of ribbon.

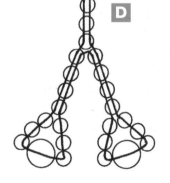

making **vintage** jewellery

loretta

loop placement

ribbon placement
(front only)

loretta

front/back

front/back lining

fold line

handle loop

madeline

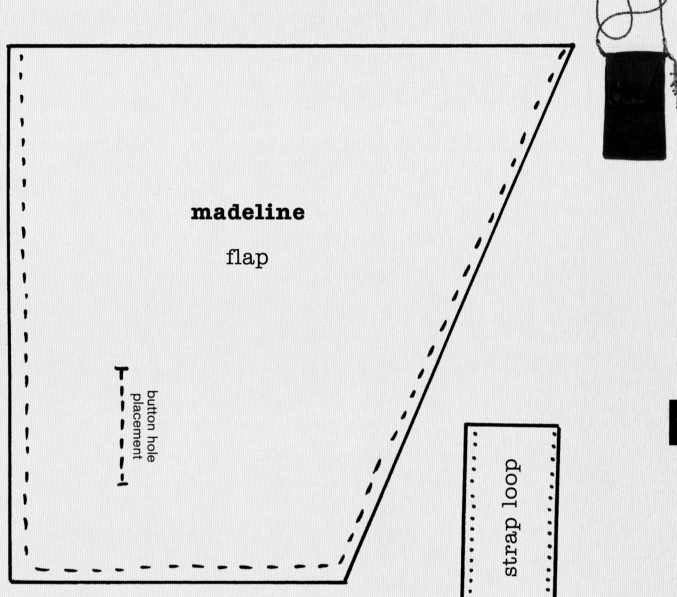

madeline

flap

button hole
placement

strap loop

madeline

front/back

front/back lining

bridget

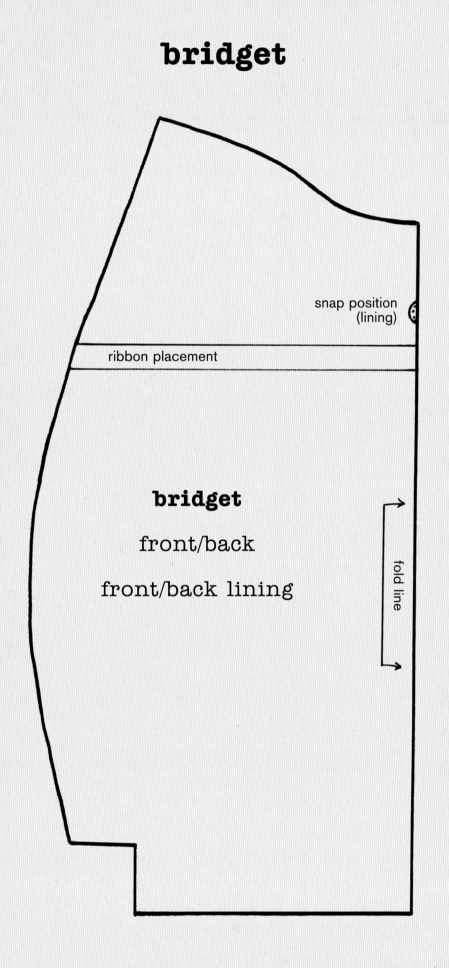

snap position
(lining)

ribbon placement

bridget

front/back

front/back lining

fold line

materials and suppliers

UK

Creative Beadcraft Limited
Unit 2,
Asheridge Road,
Cheshum,
Buckinghamshire,
HP5 2PT
Tel: (01494) 778818
www.creativebeadcraft.co.uk

Suppliers of a huge range of beads, findings, sequins and tools through mail order catalogue, retail shop and online.

Bead Exclusive
Nixon House,
119-121 Teignmouth Road,
Torquay,
Devon,
TQ1 4BG
Tel: (01803) 322000
www.beadexclusive.com

Beautiful selection of unusual beads and findings. Mail order catalogue available.

Spangles the Bead People
Carole Morris,
Spangles,
1 Casburn Lane,
Burwell,
Cambridge
CB5 0ED
Tel: (01638) 742024
www.spangles4beads.co.uk

Extremely good source for a wide range of 'beading' books, along with beads.

Panduro Hobby
Westway House,
Transport Avenue,
Brentford,
Middlesex,
TW8 9HF
Tel: 0208 8476161
www.panduro.co.uk

Suppliers of trims, beads, findings and other craft materials.

MacCulloch & Wallis
25-26 Dering Street,
London W1S 1AT
Tel: 0207 6290311
www.macculloch-wallis.co.uk

Suppliers of ribbons, buttons, feathers, beads and related items through mail order catalogue and shop.

US

Vintage Vogue,
712 June Drive,
Corona,
California,
92879 – 1143,
USA
www.vintagevogue.com

Online suppliers of velvet leaves, stamen, wool felt, silk ribbons and flower/leaf beads used in this book.

The Beadin' Path, Inc.
15, Main Street,
Freeport,
Maine 04032,
USA
www.beadinpath.com

Online suppliers of new and vintage glass beads, vintage Lucite beads, vintage pendants and unusual metal beads and components.

www.jewelrysupply.com
Jewelry Supply Order Dept.,
301 Derek Place Roseville,
CA 95678
USA

Online suppliers of everything from beads and findings to beautiful fashion related charms including handbags and shoes.

www.shipwreckbeads.com
Shipwreck Beads,
8560 Commerce Place Drive NE,
Lacey,
WA 98516, USA

Online suppliers of a big range of beads, chain, Swarovski crystals and jewellery making supplies

www.wigjig.com
WigJig,
PO Box 5124,
Gaithersburg,
MD 20882,
USA

Official WigJig website giving information on choosing a wire jig, design ideas plus online store where you can purchase jigs, wire and related materials.

Australia

OZBEADS
12, Curzon Street,
Toowoomba,
Queensland 4350
Australia
www.ozbeads.com.au

Suppliers of beads including Indian glass mixes (including the heart pendants used in the book), freshwater pearls, antique finish metal and semi-precious beads.

A & E Metal Merchants
Suite 606, 6th Floor,
89 York Street
Sydney NSW 2000,
Australia
Phone 02 8568 4200
www.aemetal.com.au

Art wires as well as jewellery findings, chain and wires in various metals including sterling silver.

Specklefarm
(Store) 111, Bridport Street,
Albert Park, Victoria 3207,
Australia
www.specklefarm.com.au

Beautiful range of own design striped grosgrain ribbons.

Also in Australia, the national chain of **Spotlight** stores stocks a huge range of craft items including everything from ribbons, beads, and jewellery findings to gift packaging.

acknowledgements

Thanks to Pamela Medlen for providing the helping hands for the step-by-step photographs. Also thanks to photographer Robert Fyfe for taking the technical shots, and for his expertise and patience.

Thanks to Will Russell for the photograph of me!

Many thanks to Clare Miller for her meticulous and supportive editing style, to Gilda Pacitti for her creative input and to Gerrie Purcell for giving me another chance to share my designs with other fans of vintage fashions around the world.

Thanks to Mark for support and patience in proofreading and to Mum and Charlie for their continued love and support from afar throughout this project.

GMC Publications would like to thank the following people for loaning props for photography:

Virginia Brehaut, Wendy Collinson, Tracy Hallett, Andrea Hargreaves, Gill Orsman, Gilda Pacitti and Gill Parris

suppliers

155

materials

index

To request a full catalogue of GMC titles, please contact:

GMC Publications, Castle Place, 166 High Street, Lewes, East Sussex BN7 1XU, United Kingdom
Tel: 01273 488005 Fax: 01273 402866
www.gmcbooks.com